INDIVIDUALS, GROUPS, AND ORGANIZATIONS BENEATH THE SURFACE

INDIVIDUALS, GROUPS, AND ORGANIZATIONS BENEATH THE SURFACE

An Introduction

Lionel F. Stapley

KARNAC

LONDON   NEW YORK

First published in 2006 by
H. Karnac (Books) Ltd.
6 Pembroke Buildings, London NW10 6RE

British Library Cataloguing in Publication Data

A C.I.P. for this book is available from the British Library

   ISBN 1 85575 319 7

Edited, designed and produced by The Studio Publishing
Services Ltd, Exeter EX4 8JN

Printed in Great Britain

10 9 8 7 6 5 4 3 2 1

www.karnacbooks.com

Contents

Contents

About the author

Lionel Stapley, MSc, PhD, is the Director of OPUS (an Organisation for Promoting Understanding of Society) and an organizational consultant. He has worked as a staff member of several international Group Relations Conferences and his consultancy clients include a variety of organizations in the public and private sectors. He publishes frequently, and is the author of *The Personality of the Organisation: A Psychodynamic Explanation of Culture and Change* (Free Association, 1996) and of *It's an Emotional Game: Learning About Leadership from the Experience of Football* (Karnac, 2002); and co-editor with Larry Gould and Mark Stein of *The Systems Psychodynamics of Organizations* (Karnac, 2001) and *Applied Experiential Learning: The Group Relations Training Approach* (Karnac, 2004).

He is the Chair of the Editorial Management Committee of the OPUS International Journal *Organisational & Social Dynamics*; a Chartered Fellow of the Chartered Institute of Personnel and Development (FCIPD), a Chartered Fellow of the Chartered Institute of Management (FCIM); and a Member of the International Society for the Psychoanalytic Study of Organisations (ISPSO).

Preface

The aim of this book is to expose and explore something of the world that exists beneath the surface of individuals, groups, organizations and institutions; to make available for consideration and meaning-making some of those aspects of our lives that are not normally within our awareness. In doing so, I shall attempt to show that although the phenomena of this world beneath the surface are not part of our conscious awareness, they nevertheless have a constant and active influence on everything we do. The part that these beneath-the-surface phenomena play has precisely the same effect as those phenomena that are part of our conscious awareness.

The subject matter of this book is experiential learning, which by its nature is continuous, dynamic, and unique to each individual and to each circumstance. In many respects, a book about experiential learning may be seen as a contradiction. To simply read about experiential phenomena will not lead to the required level of understanding of the subject matter. Therefore, I want to make it clear at this early stage that to gain a deeper understanding of this sort of learning the individual needs to adopt a reflective stance. However, the study of individuals, groups and organizations by theorists and practitioners using a mainly systems psychodynamic methodology, particularly those engaged in the Group Relations approach to learning, have helpfully identified and labelled various behaviours that occur in and between individuals and in groups and organizations. These provide a basic framework that is a valuable starting point.

Simply reading about these behaviours will not in itself enable the reader to develop a comprehensive understanding of these beneath-the-surface phenomena. But the many examples provided throughout the book and an invitation to the reader to reflect on his or her own experiences may do so. That having been said, the last thing I should want to do is to deter readers from exploring and developing knowledge of this important area of organizational behaviour, because I am convinced that it will add greatly to an understanding of their management, academic, and professional roles, no matter what they may be.

It has been said that we have a hatred of learning from experience. Unlike cognitive learning, which most frequently results only in change at an espoused level, experiential learning always involves personal change to some degree. When we speak of experiential learning we are referring to our experience, to our learning, which means that we are talking about changes within. On many occasions we may find the learning and subsequent change to be disturbing, or perhaps uncomfortable, but we will be able assimilate the changes without too much trouble. But there will be occasions when the learning is so profound and so disturbing that we will all develop the strongest resistance to the changes involved. In these instances we may need to struggle with the resulting emotions and be determined and persistent if we are to achieve an accommodation of the learning. That is, if we are indeed able to do so.

For many readers this will be new and unfamiliar territory, and while I want you to be aware that you may initially resist or reject some of the material, I would also seek to encourage you to persist through any discomfort; to take your time; and to reflect on your own experiences. I believe you will find the journey worthwhile. In the remainder of this Preface I first set the context by exploring and identifying explanations for some of the reasons why most of us don't have a sound knowledge of this material. I then distinguish the field of study by providing an introduction to the world beneath the surface through identifying the nature of the material that will be discussed throughout the book. This is followed by a brief overview of the sort of phenomena that exist beneath the surface.

Most of us appear to live unreflecting lives and to be content with simple answers to the questions surrounding experience. However, many – if not all – of us have moments of self-awareness when we find ourselves perplexed about our own behaviour, perhaps about our whole personal history. At such times we may feel that the simple answers just don't add up. Somehow, we need to look elsewhere for a deeper understanding of our experience. For example, we may feel we have been living for years in such a way as to meet the expectations of other people – of members of our family, for instance, or of our employers. We may feel that we have neglected our own wishes and purposes, or even have forgotten what we once were. In a rare moment of self-awareness we may wonder why we are driven to continually act in a certain way.

As Freud so dramatically showed in his ground-breaking work concerning 'slips of the tongue', and as we also discover when we have moments of self-awareness, there is a part of us all that is not readily apparent and frequently not accessed by us. It is a world beneath the surface that is not available to most of our perceptual processes. Unlike most of our social experience, our senses of sight, sound, smell, and touch do not provide access to this part of our world. Yet, as those moments of self-awareness show, there is a further vital and important part of us that affects all that we do.

For many readers it may seem incomprehensible that we can go through life without knowing a considerable amount about ourselves. One of the most obvious reasons, and a major consideration, is that concerning the nature of learning in our society. The predominant approach to learning in the Western world is one that is greatly influenced by centuries of philosophical and scientific thinking that demands that subjects of study be broken down into measurable units that can then be subject to tests such as those of verification and replicability: a world of quantitative analysis. This is currently reinforced by our education system, which is based upon a successful but ultimately reductionist philosophy of science. It is further reinforced in organizations where technological advances have had the effect of inadvertently reducing the humanistic aspects of management. A result is that we are greatly influenced by (the irrational) expectations that we hold as employees and managers (or citizens and politicians) that formal strategies and structures as represented by managers (or politicians) can offer the right answer (a cure) for all organizational (or societal) problems.

The dominant way of making sense of the complex organizational and societal situations that we face is by concentrating on the rational and predictable aspects of human experience. That having been said, I don't want to give the impression that in some instances and for some purposes quantitative measures are not highly appropriate. For example, a finance department in an organization, or the Treasury in government, would be failing in their task if they took a mainly qualitative view of the relevant statistics. If they were to view them, say, as good for the workforce or other beneficiaries, or better than last year, and ignore the quantitative evidence that the organization or country was going bust it would plainly be nonsensical. Or, taking a further example, if those in organizations ignored quantitative data about, say, buildings or transport and substituted their own qualitative subjective measures, this approach could also result in dire consequences. Something similar to this is alleged to have occurred in regard to the Challenger space disaster where a subjective 'group think' process predominated at the cost of ignoring important quantitative data.

From the preceding paragraph the reader might think that I am making a case for the current qualitative approach: far from it. What I believe this last example shows is that whether we are aware of it or not, subjectivity cannot be ignored even in situations where quantitative approaches are appropriate and even vital. No matter what the circumstances, people are involved in the process and, consequently, we need to be aware of researcher subjectivity (or bias), which is always likely to have an effect on the findings. But I want to go further than this because, while accepting that the dominant approach may be appropriate in certain circumstances, there are others where such an approach is totally inappropriate. This is particularly so in matters concerning human behaviour where, in addition to data that is available to us through our usual processes of perception, we also need to consider material arising from our internal world. In moving the discussion forward it may help to distinguish in general terms the sort of learning we are talking about.

Most of the rational or surface learning is what we might refer to as 'learning about' or cognitive learning. From an early age we are introduced to 'learning about' all manner of things that will be useful, perhaps even essential, to us throughout our lives. Starting with our mother teaching us the alphabet and simple mathematics, we then move on to school, where we are taught an expanding and gradually more complex further set of subject matters. On leaving school we either go to some form of further education or go direct to the workplace. Whenever we reach the workplace, we are then taught what might be referred to as 'industry or discipline specific' knowledge and skills, which may include management training. A result is that by the time we become adults we have achieved a degree of learning about matters that can be shared with various individuals and groups within our society.

However, when we reflect carefully on our lives, we will realize that, while less obvious, there is another sort of learning that also starts from our earliest days: that which we may refer to as 'learning from experience'. This learning also initially develops out of the relationship with the mother. This sort of learning occurs beneath the surface, within the individual, and it concerns the development of what may be referred to as internal mental objects. These include, among other things, developed defence mechanisms that enable us to cope with painful experiences; developed values that include a sense of what is right and what is wrong – our conscience; the unconscious; and emotional responses. Each of these phenomena bring

their own complications, but at this stage it will be sufficient to simply label them and consider them as internalized objects that are important and significant parts of
every individual. At various points in the book all of these
issues are referred to in considerable detail.

An awareness of this different sort of learning and
knowledge may be a helpful beginning in developing an
understanding of our general ignorance of beneath-the-
surface phenomena. Another approach that will lift the
veil of understanding is to view human behaviour as a
psycho-social process. The concept of 'psycho-social'
draws attention to the fact that what we are dealing with
in social systems is two distinct levels at the same time.
That is, we need to conceptualize a group, an organization, or society as a process of human behaviour that is
both psychological and social at the same time. At the
'social' level we need to analyse technological, economic,
sociological and political factors: the products and services
the group, organization, or society provides; and the organizational structures, strategies, and procedures that
management or politicians have created, which together
comprise the everyday life of the organization or society.
Those aspects of the processes of human behaviour may
be regarded as the 'external' realities of the members of the
organization. These are the rational aspects of society and
organizations and these are what we have referred to as
'knowing about'.

This level is frequently the full extent of our knowledge
and understanding – the rational and seemingly
predictable aspects of human behaviour. But, of course,
that's not all there is to human behaviour. As well as the
social level we also need to consider the ever-present
psychological level of human behaviour. At the 'psycho'

level we are talking about the subjective experience of members of a group, organization, or society: about what goes on in the minds of members of the group, organization, or society. This may include the ideas and ways of thinking about how they perceive the external realities in relation to how they behave or act. Their actions will be influenced by their beliefs, values, hopes, anxieties, and the defence mechanisms that they employ. Put another way, we are referring to the 'internal' realities of the members of the organization. These are the irrational and perhaps unconscious aspects of us all and these are influenced by what we have referred to as 'knowledge of experience'.

These two levels – the external and internal worlds of people – are in continual interaction: what goes on in the minds of people is partly reactive to what happens around them, but is also very much proactive. People's ideas and ways of thinking influence the way they act upon their surroundings to bring about change in them. This is all part and parcel of the dynamic processes. These different types of knowledge are also important in understanding how individuals develop an understanding of their world. We make meaning out of our experiences, and experience itself is at the boundary between the two worlds – external interaction and internal interpretation. We experience the group, organization, or societal environment through our perceptive processes and filter them down and match them against a pool of internalized knowledge and feelings consisting of our past experience. The various identities that we take will affect our perceptive filters, as will the environments that we are a part of. In this way, our own subjective processes affect the way we determine reality. Each experience will be shaped by the individual's previous experience.

Throughout the book I shall make frequent references to, and use of, psychoanalytic theory, which is deeply committed to the conviction that how these inherited characteristics will be shaped depends on a person's life experience. Thus, it subscribes to a historical view, according to which later events are to a considerable degree conditioned by what has happened before. Therefore, the earliest history of the individual is of the greatest importance in respect to what they will be like in their later life, not only because it is the basis for all that follows but also because early history largely determines how later life will be experienced. While genetic and evolutionary history creates an individual's potentialities, their early personal history, more than anything that follows, accounts for the forms these potentialities will take in the actuality of their life.

In seeking to provide an introduction to the sort of phenomena occurring beneath the surface, the most obvious point of departure is the individual. Beneath the surface every individual is unique. While we may share some similarities, none of us is a 'clone' of another. We all start life in a truly dependent state and our early experience of authority figures will have a lasting impression on the way that we take up roles in groups, organizations, or society. Even though some of us may have had the same parents, or were brought up in the same street, or went to the same school, or the same workplace, each of us will have had a life experience different from anyone else. In all manner of ways, rather like our fingerprints or DNA, there is something quite unique about us all. That's why we could never write a book about human behaviour that treats all experiences the same. Only in the most general of terms could such processes be the subject of confirmation and validation. Not only is each of us unique, but each interaction is also unique.

I described above the way that psychoanalytic theory subscribes to a historical view, according to which later events are, to a considerable degree, conditioned by what has happened before. The reader may not be surprised, therefore, that the primary experience between infant and mother is at the heart of much that influences the world beneath the surface. The earliest history of the individual is of the greatest importance in respect to what they will be like in their later life, not only because it is the basis for all that follows, but also because early history largely determines how later life will be experienced. The experiences arising during this stage of life lead to the development of various phenomena that will be referred to throughout the book.

This has implications for the way that we perceive sensory data. The totality of this learning (our pool of internalized knowledge and feelings) is something that we all develop but is something that is unique to each individual and affects all human relationships. The world we respond to, the world that our behaviour is directed towards, is the world as we symbolize it, or represent it to ourselves. Changes in the actual world must be followed by changes in our representation of it if they are to affect our expectations, and hence, our subsequent behaviour. We look at the world in the light of what we have learned to expect from our past experience of the world. We put objects that to us are similar into the same category, even though we can perceive differences among them. Without such patterns the world would appear to be such an undifferentiated homogeneity that we would be unable to make any sense of it. In such circumstances, even a poor fit is more helpful than nothing at all.

We also need to be aware that human beings are not only capable of experiencing external data, they can also develop internal concepts. In our development process, before speech there is no conception, only perception and a readiness to act according to the enticements of the perceived world. It is by means of symbols that we form concepts. This is a remarkable advance, because once we have a concept of a piece of reality we can play with it, think about it and, most importantly, relate it to other pieces. Because of our ability to form concepts we can construct an object in the mind that is a non-human object. This complicates our meaning-making activity considerably because we may now be relating to something that no other human being is aware of.

Another area of particular interest is meaning-making at the 'emotional' level. Faced with any experience, the emotional learning that life has given us, such as the memory of a past disastrous relationship, sends signals that streamline our decision-making process by eliminating some options and highlighting others at the outset. In this way the emotions are involved in reasoning – as is the thinking brain. It is recognized that within the individual strong feelings come to be bound up into systems and sub-systems that have been called complexes, defences, conflicts, attitudes, and so on. All of these influence and determine a person's behaviour in the relationships of everyday life.

Yet another aspect is meaning-making at the unconscious level. As was first discovered by Freud, the unconscious mind consists mainly of repressed sentiments that have their foundations in infancy. By repression is meant the exclusion of painful and unpleasant material from consciousness. In this way, mental tendencies and traces of past experiences that once acted in full consciousness are now present only in our unconscious. However, this does not mean that they are completely gone. On the contrary, even though unconscious they still exist, and these past experiences may affect our behaviour without entering consciousness.

From the foregoing we may be convinced that there is a largely unknown and seldom referred to part of our lives, a sort of 'parallel world', that is as important and influential as that which we are constantly aware of. We may also be convinced that the value-free, value-neutral, value-avoiding model of science that was inherited from physics, chemistry, and astronomy is quite unsuitable when we extend science to the extreme difficulties of biological behaviour, human emotion and social organization. This inevitably means that we need to eschew our previously accepted approach and open our thinking to other possibilities. In our search for an alternative approach, we need to adopt a methodology that will enable us to consider not only the more obvious and rational processes that are occurring in society, but also the irrational processes that are occurring 'beneath the surface'; those irrational processes that we are not normally aware of, or, if we are aware of them, don't fully understand.

To continue to view organizational and societal activity from the monocular perspective of only one part of our knowledge (knowledge about), while ignoring the other perspective (learning from experience), is as important as, say, the management equivalent of not taking into consideration financial implications of organizations. To be effective we need to employ the binocular perspective of both types of learning. However, other than for the purposes of clarity, I do not intend to refer to the more rational aspects of human behaviour in this book. Rather, the concentration will be on a 'different' way of learning, the irrational processes, the 'psycho' or internal processes, and the way that this impacts on the more formal processes of organization.

In searching for a means of understanding we might make the mistake of exploring one or other of the social sciences that have a long record of studying human behaviour. It will soon be realized that the historical division into the various disciplines has only served to exacerbate the problem. Some branches of sociology and anthropology take the social as the unit of study and ignore the individual. Or, put another way, they study only the social and ignore the psychological level. Some branches of psychology take the opposite route, taking the individual as the unit of study without considering the social context. In other words, they study only the psychological and ignore the social level. An added problem is that each is likely to claim that theirs is the fundamental science. As I hope I have shown, albeit briefly, everything is embedded in the social context of individuals' lives, particularly the dominant primary group, the family. But it is only the functioning of individual minds that make the human collectively possible. Language, culture, and all the other rules by which we live are achievements of the species, not individuals. But without human minds, neither language, nor culture, nor rules could exist. It is really a social psychology.

Being a social psychology, psychoanalytic theory provides a means of studying the phenomena under review. Such theory has been used for the study of live objects that are seen, experienced, and recognized subjectively in contrast to the traditional sciences, which study 'objects only'. The application of psychoanalytic theory to organizations and social science in general has a history going back well over fifty years – perhaps as long as a century. Some readers may feel that this puts them at a disadvantage, because they fear they may have difficulty comprehending some of the concepts referred to. I would seek to allay any such fears, as all such references are used in a context that will enable a greater appreciation of what is being said. It is also hoped that this book will continue the process of making psycho-dynamic theory more accessible to a greater proportion of society than currently exists.

Perhaps this is an appropriate point to repeat my previous warning. The sort of phenomena that we are referring to here cannot be learned solely from reading books. This is largely subjective material that only those involved at the time can fully understand. All that I can do in this book is to expose some of the behaviours that have been identified by social scientists using a psychodynamic frame, as occurring in individuals, groups, organizations and institutions at various times. On many occasions such behaviours have been identified as occurring when those individuals and members of groups are experiencing high levels of anxiety or other emotions.

So, how do we access this world beneath the surface? No matter what our human experiences are they always go beyond our particular methods of understanding at any given moment. There is no methodology that will provide a complete and satisfactory explanation of our behaviour and the best way that we can gain an understanding of our identity as a self is to look into our experience. We cannot make use of our perceptual senses of sight, sound, smell, and touch, but we can get in touch with our emotions. As human beings we can reflect on some past experience and can picture ourselves as doing something, and we can then also experience the feelings that we had when we were actually doing whatever it was. By self-reflection we can develop self-awareness that provides access to this world beneath the surface.

If this Preface has served as a means of causing you to start to become a 'reflective citizen', you will have begun the task of re-introducing yourself to yourself. By self-reflection you will have begun the task of developing self-awareness. Being reflective citizens means that we will not only be aware of the rational processes, we shall also begin to understand the irrational, sometimes unconscious processes that are occurring beneath the surface; processes that are having such an important affect on our lives and on our societies. What we might term a parallel world, a different world, not so obvious but every bit as influential.

The structure of this book reflects the belief that if we are to understand group, organizational, and institutional behaviour we need to consider the processes and dynamics that occur at three different levels: what we do as individuals; what we do in relationships; and what we do in groups. These three distinct but progressive and inter-related Sections, which each deal with one of the levels referred to, are used to expose and explore beneath-the-surface processes and dynamics that occur in all groups, organizations and institutions.

In the first Section I expose and explore the way that individual processes and dynamics will have an impact on group, organizational, and institutional dynamics. In this Section I take the view that the individual is the primary building block in all human activity and that no matter what the activity, be it concerning relationships or groups, an understanding of the individual must be at the heart of our exploration. As is the case in real life, the individual provides a base from which we can explore relationships and groups. This is a valuable Section in terms of setting things in a context and in exposing and exploring the pivotal role that the individual plays in the process of meaning-making. Everything referred to in this Section will be relevant to relationships, groups, organizations, and institutions. Those with little knowledge of beneath-the-surface processes may find this Section useful for reference purposes, especially when referring to the material in Sections Two and Three.

Without an understanding of the beneath-the-surface activities of the individual we could not begin to understand groups, organizations, or institutions. The approach taken is that the individual is the meaning-maker and that he or she develops a pool of internalized knowledge and feelings that is compared with sense data in the environment to produce meaning. Beneath-the-surface processes that help the individual to make sense of his or her world, and those that we use to help us deal with unbearable thoughts and feelings, become part of our internal world. These processes are explored in sub-sections on the following aspects: classifying and conceptualizing reality; boundaries; conflict; attitudes and values; emotions; repression; defence mechanisms; splitting, projection and introjection; displacement, and scapegoating; and creativity.

Section Two explores the way that relational phenomena add to individual dynamics to have an additional impact on group, organization, and institutional dynamics. In this Section I take the view that when we enter into relationships with another individual or group, further beneath-the-surface phenomena are evoked that, unless they are exposed and understood, may create the unhelpful formation of firm boundaries that prevent progression. Some of the affects and dynamics that occur when entering into relationships with others are explored in sub-sections on the following aspects: politics; boundaries; the politics of identity; power and authority; reality and phantasy; relationships; trust; and relatedness.

In the final Section, on Groups, I expose and explore the further level of study, that of group dynamics. This Section is intended to take the reader to a different level of beneath-the-surface behaviour that is specific to groups. Although heavily influenced by individual processes and dynamics, this is a level of understanding that considers groups 'as if' they were an organism with a group mind. This requires that we go beyond taking the group at face value and viewing actions by individuals as actions they have carried out on behalf of the group. The Section includes an extensive introduction that explains the group-as-a-whole approach and continues with sub-sections on: culture; social systems as a defence against anxiety; basic assumption behaviour; and systems.

The Afterword is intended to provide an opportunity to expose and explore some of the ways that we can develop a capacity to become a more reflective citizen. It will particularly seek to raise awareness that our feelings and emotions have as great an influence on our lives as do our thought processes. And that, in many instances, the activity of being a person – that of meaning-making – may evoke deep and unconscious feelings that are primitive and aggressive in nature. Consequently, if we are to access and gain an understanding of beneath-the-surface activity, we need to develop a sophisticated level of self-awareness that enables us to control and manage our feelings.

This book is intended to be of interest to anyone who wishes to gain a deeper understanding of themselves and the part that they play in influencing family, group, organizational, and societal dynamics. It will be of interest for those who are thoughtful enough to want to gain a better understanding of the processes of life in general. It will be an important text for academics and students of courses on organizational behaviour, organizational development, group dynamics, human resources, and other management studies; for those who are practising managers and leaders in all manner of organizations; and to anthropologists, sociologists, political scientists, and other social scientists who may wish to extend their thinking and awareness beyond the traditional way of thinking of their specific discipline. And it will be of interest to those practitioners who are involved with providing a service that concerns them in understanding different parts of society. These may include nurses, doctors, health workers, social workers, probation officers, police officers, prison officers, and many others.

Acknowledgements

I want to express my gratitude and to acknowledge the immense influence that colleagues and participants in various scientific fora have had on the writing of this book by helping me develop knowledge and practice of the world beneath the surface. For over ten years, as the Director of OPUS – an Organisation for Promoting Understanding of Society – I have been privileged during many Scientific Meetings, Listening Posts, and experiential workshops to share the thinking of some of the

leading theorists and practitioners of a systems psychodynamic approach to the study of organizations and society.
Over a similar period, through membership of the
International Society for the Psychoanalytic Study of
Organisations (ISPSO) I have also had the privilege of
sharing the thinking of many who are at the cutting edge
of theoretical and practical application of a systems
psychodynamic approach to organizations. These good
friends and colleagues have been very influential in helping me to develop the views expressed in this book.

Over a longer period I have also had the benefit of
learning from my many clients, who are a constant source
of inspiration and learning and without whom this book
could not have been written. I should also like to thank
Andrew Collie and Jina Barrett for their helpful
comments on an earlier draft. And Leena Hakkinen of
Karnac for the encouraging, patient, and supportive
manner in which she took up her editorial function.

SECTION ONE

INDIVIDUALS

If we were taking a more traditional approach we might well be seeking assurances that by developing formal structures, policies and strategies, and providing management training for organizational members we would very likely be successful: or, put another way, we would get it right. But for most of us our experience will be that in spite of the many books that we have read; the many courses we have attended; and the many changes we have made; the organizations we have been concerned with have still not been successful and some may have failed completely. Even when we have selected those that we perceived to be the best personnel and provided them with attractive terms and conditions and some of the best working conditions, many of us still didn't get the success we planned for in the organizations concerned.

For those who are experienced and qualified managers or professionals this can be a confusing and worrying situation. In many instances their knowledge and learning may have helped them to respond to situations in an effective manner, but now it's all going wrong. At this stage I would ask you to consider the possibility that there are other phenomena that impact on these organizations: those that are far from obvious; more difficult to understand; and not available from the usual management

1

books and courses. Perhaps also 'getting it right' may not be possible in many circumstances and that even getting it right to a good enough degree requires that, in addition to the formal procedures, we also require an understanding of beneath-the-surface phenomena that occur in all groups, organizations, and institutions. When we take such an approach we may discover that these beneath-the-surface phenomena are some of the reasons why organizations have not been entirely successful.

Getting to a position where we can begin to understand the influence that beneath-the-surface processes have on groups, organizations, and institutions depends on how we view them. If we can only see things as they are presented to us, what we might refer to as their face value, we may simply see awkward people and helpful people; or we may see only structures and strategies. But that is to ignore those processes that will be exposed in this book. If we view groups, organizations, and institutions as processes of human behaviour we see other things. With this added information we may now begin to try to understand why an individual is seemingly awkward or helpful. Or why what was considered by senior management to be a rational, sensible, organizational structure was being rejected by the workforce, and why other planned changes were facing hostility. It is this way of looking that we shall concentrate on in this book.

In this Section, I begin the process by exposing and exploring the way that beneath-the-surface processes and dynamics concerning individuals will have an impact on group, organizational, and institutional dynamics. I take the view that the individual is the primary building block in all human activity and that no matter what the activity, be it concerning relationships or groups, an understanding of the individual must be at the heart of our exploration. Starting with the individual, as is the case in real life, provides a base from which we can explore relationships and groups. And, I would suggest, without an understanding of the beneath-the-surface activities of the individual we could not begin to understand groups, organizations, or institutions.

As human beings we are constantly engaged in the process of meaning-making – that's what humans do. Seen in the light of our normal sense data – sight, sound, smell and touch – we can generally understand this concept. We know that different people sometimes make different interpretations of material presented to them. Indeed, we may even be generous and accept that for the person involved 'perception is reality'. In addition, we can always check with them how they are viewing some particular shared sense data. But things are more complicated when we take a deeper look at our average human being. It may seem a strange notion, but it is important to understand that there is no such thing as just an individual. The truth is that we are all part of a group from earliest infancy. In the earliest days the mother provides the context in which development takes place, and from the point of view of the new-born she is part of the self. There is no such thing as a baby, only a mother-and-baby field. Indeed, the substance of the object relations argument in psychoanalysis, and one that I share, is that the dominating feature of human psychology is an impulse to form relationships – a social orientation. From the early relation of the mother and child in the maternal holding environment a relationship grows through the ability of both parties to experience and adjust to each other's natures.

The individual is the dominant element in the meaning-making process and he or she develops a pool of internalized knowledge and feelings that is compared with sense data in the environment to produce meaning. Beneath-the-surface processes that help the individual to make sense of his or her world and those that we use to help us deal with unbearable thoughts and feelings, become part of our internal world. In all instances these processes will have an impact on group, organizational, and institutional dynamics.

1. Introduction: never just an individual – but an individual is the primary building block in all human activity

Without reflection individuals may be inclined to accept readily presented explanations for many aspects of human experience. The fact that important explanations are subsequently clearly identified as without good foundation doesn't seem to stop human beings proceeding in this manner. Perhaps a highly relevant example might concern the use of psychoanalysis as a social science. Over a hundred years have passed since psychoanalysis was first introduced to the world. Since that time, there have been many developments and clarifications that have resulted in it becoming a largely accepted discipline that has proved its value as a theory and practice that is beneficial to understanding human behaviour. Yet, many social science disciplines fail to reflect on their practice in the light of that information, relying instead on readily presented explanations.

A further important example is the notion referred to above: that there is no such thing as 'just an individual'. For the sake of clarity I may from time to time refer to individuals and groups as if they were capable of analysis as isolated individuals or groups, while this is clearly not the case. From birth onwards we are in a constant state of relatedness to various other individuals and groups. As a child we are dependent on our mother for our very survival and for our psychological well-being. Indeed, there is never 'just a mother': she is influenced by her relatedness to the child and responds to both the child's physical and psychological needs. There is a mutual influence

5

between mother and child and this process continues with other people throughout our lives.

We can be related to others by virtue of a whole host of reasons. For example, we could be related as fellow professionals or work colleagues or we could be related as members of a church or other social grouping. These are fairly typical and obvious forms of social relatedness. But, as with the mother and infant, a state of relatedness is both psychological and social. We may helpfully describe relatedness as the processes of mutual influence between individual and individual, between individual and group, group and group, and group and organization. Beyond that we might consider the relatedness of organization and the wider society. Social relatedness is important, but much more interesting to our current purposes is our psychological relatedness to other individuals or groups.

The process of mutual influence between individuals is an ongoing process that will have an affect on nearly everything we do. For example, the feelings and phantasies that we have about another individual will have a huge impact on the way we engage with that other individual. For example, a client who was a middle manager referred to his senior manager by saying 'She doesn't like me'. When I enquired why, he told me that some weeks earlier he had submitted a report to the senior manger that she clearly felt was rubbish and had since not been in contact. When I explored this with him, he reflected that this view was one based on his feelings and phantasies and that he needed to speak with the senior manager to establish what had happened. When I next saw him he cheerfully told me that his senior manager had quite liked the report and had not taken action on it to date because of other matters that would affect it. They actually had a very good relationship.

There is no escape from relatedness. Even if, as adults, we sit alone in the isolation of our own homes contemplating some problem or issue, we are never alone in our minds. We are still linked to many others in a state of relatedness and this will have an affect on our contemplation. The notion of relatedness serves to remind us that we cannot ignore the fact that everything is embedded in the social context of individuals' lives, particularly the dominant primary group, the family. In any given situation in a group or organization we are in a state of relatedness to others, and this will result in mutual influence between individuals and groups. It will be helpful for the reader to reflect on the notion of relatedness throughout the book, even though I may be referring to individual or group activity. However, we also need to bear in mind the equally important notion that it is only the functioning of individual minds that make the human collectively possible. Without human minds, neither language, nor culture, nor rules could exist. Consequently, while we are referring to a social psychology, we need to understand something of the way the individual makes sense of meaning.

Among students of the social sciences there have always been those who have recognized the fact that some knowledge of the human mind and of its modes of operation is an essential part of their equipment, and that the successful development of the social sciences must be dependent upon such knowledge. As will have been gathered from the Preface, I very much share this view. I shall, therefore, be continuing from the notion that the self is the organizing function within the individual and the function by means of which one human being can relate to another.

No matter what the circumstances, we as individuals play the central role in making sense of our experiences.

The notion that we constitute reality rather than somehow happen upon it may seem strange to non-reflective citizens who are more inclined to be content with simple answers to the questions surrounding experience. As has been said, in the non-reflective world taking things at their face value may result in our seeing only formal structures, policies, and strategies, or awkward and helpful people, as if they were existing facts. But when we reflect on the processes that occur in coming to the conclusion that someone is an awkward person, we come to realize that this may not be so. As an example, let's assume that 'Peter', who could be a doctor in a hospital or manager in a factory, is regarded as an awkward person. As will be more fully explained below, as individuals we do not simply take in all the sense data we become aware of. Our perceptive processes act as a filter that lets through some sense data and ignores others. To put it simply, in the case of 'Peter' we may be so annoyed by the activities we see as awkward that we filter out all other information, some of which may portray Peter in a good light. In this way, we are totally involved in the meaning-making process and from one aspect of behaviour we label 'Peter' as an awkward person.

To be more accurate, the situation is not that a person makes meaning; rather, the activity of being a person is the activity of meaning-making. If we reflect carefully on the process, we can appreciate that there is no feeling, no experience, no thought, no perception independent of a meaning-making context in which it becomes a feeling, an experience, a thought, a perception, because we human beings are the meaning-making context. Without human activity these phenomena simply would not exist. If we, as human beings, did not take in our various sensations and translate them into something they would not be what they are. Thus, we may say that human being is an activity. It is not about the doing that a human does, it is about the doing which a human is.

We can also say that as human beings we are constantly engaged in the process of meaning-making and that personality is a dynamic process. This concerns all sorts of knowledge, including cognitive knowledge and experiential knowledge such as conception, emotions, and the unconscious, which all have their origins in the private (inner) world of a human individual. Thus, to return to Peter, if we are the meaning-makers in the process of seeing him as an 'awkward' person, it may well be the case that it is our experience that is influencing the decision and not so much Peter's demeanour. This is an important level of exploration and understanding, not only because of the basic meaning making role of the individual but also because it affects individual processes and dynamics, especially those occurring beneath the surface, which have a considerable impact on relationships and groups.

Before proceeding to an explanation of various processes that will help us to gain a deeper understanding of the individual it may be helpful to consider the characteristics of personality. In brief, we can say that 'personality' may be characterized by the following:

1. It is a psycho-social process.
2. It is evidenced by sameness and continuity.
3. It is influenced by conscious and unconscious processes.
4. It is unique for each individual.

9

5. It is a dynamic process.
6. It is such that the individual will produce forms of behaviour which will be psychologically advantageous to him or her under the conditions imposed by the environment.

These characteristics may be usefully held in mind when we are concerned with detailed explorations of different concepts.

In the following sub-sections I will explore some of the important aspects of the world beneath the surface that will impact upon our meaning-making. These may be conveniently categorized as those that help us make sense of our world; and those that we use to help us deal with unbearable thoughts and feelings. I shall start with a very basic activity, that of classifying and conceptualizing reality. This is such a frequent activity, we might even say a continuous activity, that we may seldom give it a second thought. However, as will be shown, it is a highly subjective process that has considerable implications for everything we do.

Making sense of our world

2. Classifying and conceptualizing reality

A quick reflection on our experience of every moment of every day will enable us to understand just how multi-faceted and extensive it is. To make things more difficult, every moment and every experience is unique and unrepeatable. This means that unless we are able to classify our experience on some basis of similarity we will be unable to make sense of that experience. Without some sort of categorization we would be imprisoned in the uniqueness of the here and now. The reduction of experience into some familiar form of categories is therefore essential.

Through the process of classification and naming of this world of infinite variability we are able to ensure some continuity and thus make sense out of this highly complex experience. But, of course, this is a highly selective process. We do not live in a world where we discriminate among all the possible sensory stimuli in our environment, nor do we react to each stimulus as if it were new and foreign. In effect we choose to ignore many of those perceptual differences that make each object unique. The system that we mainly choose to use for this is naming.

From this we will appreciate that the objects of our world do not present themselves to us ready classified. The categories into which they are divided are categories into which we divide them. Put another way, as human beings we are constantly engaged in the process of meaning-making – that's what humans do. When we distinguish one class of things or actions from another we are creating artificial boundaries in a field that is naturally continuous. In principle these created boundaries have no dimensions, yet they are regarded as if they were real by all of us.

By way of explanation we might take the simple example of dogs. At the two extremes people view dogs either as lovely, fluffy, cuddly animals that are regarded as 'man's best friend'; or as nasty, vicious, fearsome creatures that should be avoided. Depending on our own particular and unique experiences we will all categorize dogs somewhere on the scale from man's best friend to fearsome creatures. The fact that the particular dog that is now being experienced shows nothing of the characteristics attributed to it is largely irrelevant to our meaning-making process. The created categories we have divided dogs into and that we then continue to use are what we consider to be real. And this, of course, is precisely the way we determined and categorized Peter as 'awkward'.

The world we respond to, the world towards which our behaviour is directed, is the world as we symbolize it, or represent it to ourselves. Changes in the actual world must be followed by changes in our representation of it if they are to affect our expectations and, hence, our subsequent behaviour. We look at the world in the light of what we have learned to expect from our past experience of the world. We put objects that to us are similar into the same category, even though we can perceive differences among them. Let's return to the example of dogs, and consider a situation where a particular dog which is the object currently perceived may appear to be a cuddly, man's best friend. However, our previous experience has been that dogs are ferocious beasts. Consequently, we shall continue to categorize this and all other dogs in that way. That is, unless we continually experience dogs as cuddly and friendly, in which case we may change our categorization of dogs. Without such patterns the world would appear to be such an undifferentiated homogeneity that we would be unable to make any sense of it. In such circumstances, even a poor fit may be more helpful than nothing at all.

By the use of words and language we impose a scheme for classifying and conceptualizing our reality. This scheme of things has been referred to by several authors who have commented on the 'taken for granted' nature of language. However, the fact that we, who are familiar with our symbols, do not have to think about them when we think with them should not hide the fact that all these symbols have to be supported by a vast intellectual structure. This structure is composed of the stock of knowledge that results in our perceived reality. Because the symbolic representation is as the members of a particular society have learned to experience it, we can appreciate that words are used differently in different societies, or parts of societies. Sometimes, the result may be that language may not be a means of communication but rather a barrier to such communication.

A classic example concerned the introduction of computers. At one stage the symbolic representation of the processes were quite unlike anything that many of us had previously known. The younger members of society, being relatively unencumbered by 'old' knowledge, were able to quickly develop an understanding of the language and words used for classifying the various computer processes, whereas older people who sought to match the data against their internal pool of knowledge found it near impossible, or made classifications that were inappropriate. Thus, for many, language was a barrier to communication about computers. This may also be the case between members of different disciplines. Where, for example, a member of one discipline views human behaviour from a social perspective; and a member of a different discipline views human behaviour from a psychological perspective, there are almost bound to be barriers to communication.

As has been explained, the self plays the central role in making sense of an individual's surrounding experience. One of the processes of meaning-making is perception, which is not as simple as our everyday usage would have us believe. By the process of perception we impose some structure on new input, compare it with a pool of old information, and then either add to it or eliminate it. This pool of old information is rather like the memory of a computer; however, this is a highly sophisticated computer that is able to compare and recall vast amounts of data instantly. It is composed of a stock of knowledge developed throughout our lifetime and this is supported by a vast intellectual framework. And, in consideration of this process, we need to bear in mind that this stock of knowledge is unique to each individual.

The notion of a pool of old information is vital to understanding the process of perception. We look at our world in the light of what we have learned to expect from our past experience of the world. Surrounding experience is made sense of – internally and without conscious thought – by comparing it with our existing (internal) knowledge. This gives credence to the important psychoanalytic notion that the earliest history of the individual is of the greatest importance in respect to what they will be like in their later life, not only because it is the basis for all that follows but also because early history largely determines how later life will be experienced. The way that we, as individuals, will respond to any situation will depend greatly on the given situation as we have learned to perceive it.

To clarify, it may help if we explore the object relations argument that the dominating feature of human psychology is the impulse to form relationships. The first objects we encounter are the mother and other family members. As with objects that we classify as dogs, we also classify and categorize human objects in different ways. Thus, in simple terms, a mother may be categorized as loving and kind while a father may be categorized as cruel and heartless. From this point onwards, when we experience other women authority figures we may categorize them also as loving, kind, and generally helpful; while conversely, when we experience other male authority figures they may be categorized as cruel, heartless, and not to be trusted. From the perspective of a manager who is treated in this way, it may be a very confusing situation. Reflecting back we may now be able to gain a better understanding of the way we determined that Peter was an awkward person.

In the last few paragraphs, I have referred to sense data that could be compared with our pool of knowledge to enable the development of some form of categorization. But there is also a further aspect concerning perception, which arises when it is totally new sense data and no match (not even a bad one) is found in our existing pool of knowledge. We can only make judgements about whether we like or dislike something if it is something that we know. Our sensations must be completed by some form of appraisal before we can decide whether it is good or bad for us. The way that we, as individuals, will respond in this situation will depend on how we have learned to perceive new information. For each of us the response will be affected by our experience from childhood onwards.

As will be appreciated, precisely how an individual makes meaning is a highly subjective process. Each of us, being a unique individual possessed of a unique pool of internal knowledge; a pool of knowledge developed from birth to present day; will conceptualize and categorize data in a unique way. What goes on beneath the surface, out of our awareness, may result in different individuals making quite different meaning out of similar experiences. In terms of hard data, like buildings and computers, there may be less chance of different meanings among different people. However, once we become involved in the world of soft data, such as personality and individual behaviour, there is much greater chance of conflicting views being developed by different individuals. This sort of data is likely to trigger emotional factors in our pool of knowledge that will add a whole new perspective to the way we categorize our experiences.

It might not be unusual that two or more different individuals, having the same experience and both having compared the data with their pool of internal knowledge and feelings, have developed categories that are totally opposed to each other. To return to the previous example, from our experience we may categorize some people as helpful people and others as awkward people. A different individual, when comparing their sense data with their pool of internal knowledge and feelings might categorize some of those people we see as helpful as awkward and vice versa. By this process of categorization we create a boundary that includes what we mean by helpful and another around what we mean, or understand, by awkward. By developing different classifications or categories we automatically engage in the process of creating boundaries. In the following sub-section I begin to look at the important notion of boundaries, which will be referred to again in several different ways throughout this book.

3. Boundaries

To summarize, we have a need to classify and categorize the world as we experience it. Without some system of making sense out of total chaos the uniqueness of the here

and now would be intolerable. By classification and categorization we make the world of infinite variability bear-
able. The objects of our world do not present themselves
to us ready classified; the categories into which they are
divided are categories that we have created. When we use
symbols to distinguish one class of things or actions from
another we are creating artificial boundaries in a field that
is naturally continuous. In principle the created boundaries have no dimensions yet they are experienced as real
for you and me.

A typical example of creating artificial boundaries in a
naturally continuous field concerns human behaviour. We
might helpfully reflect on the sort of occasion where we
have attended a meeting with our manager who, of
course, we know reasonably well, but some of the others
present at the meeting do not know him at all. After the
meeting those others may say to you something like 'Your
boss is a bit of a tyrant isn't he?' To which you might reply
'No, he's OK when you know him, he's just a bit uptight
today.' Seen from our perspective this is but a part of a
continuous field. Seen from the perspective of the new-
comers their only experience of the manager is at this
meeting. As a result of this experience they create an artificial boundary by seeing the manager as 'a bit of a tyrant'.

A further example might concern an employee who at
a particular moment doesn't easily agree with decisions
made and imposed on her by management. In the continuous practice as an employee this person is regarded as a
highly satisfactory worker. However, as a means of making
sense out of the chaotic situation that has developed the
manager may categorize the individual as awkward. In
doing so the manager distinguishes this person from
others who are generally regarded as helpful and creates an

artificial boundary around her. Seen in a different manner, this individual may have been the only person with the foresight and understanding to point out the weaknesses in the management decision. The danger is that once the boundary has been drawn in this way the manager is unlikely to hear what she has to contribute.

We can helpfully distinguish three types of boundaries: spatial, temporal, and psychological. Spatial boundaries are those that are formed around territory. Some examples of artificially created spatial boundaries are neighbouring gardens and national frontiers. Temporal boundaries are those concerning time and a clear and obvious example is the segmentation of time into hours and minutes. A further example is social time, which is similarly segmented as an individual moves from one social status to another in a series of discontinuous leaps. All of these are examples of artificially created boundaries. Because this process of categorization is part of our learned and lived experience of an ordered society we might find it very difficult to live without them. However, I would stress that this makes them no less artificial.

I don't propose to further explore the matter of spatial and temporal boundaries other than to say that a reflection on them does provide helpful insights into the way that we make meaning. It does seem, though, that we need to develop boundaries for our own comfort and well-being. Therefore this concept is helpful when we turn to the third category, psychological boundaries. Something very simple happens when we answer the question 'Who am I?' when we are explaining or describing or even just inwardly feeling our 'self'; what we are actually doing, whether we know it or not, is drawing a mental line or boundary across the whole field of our experience, and everything on the inside of that boundary we are feeling or calling our 'self' while everything outside that boundary we feel to be 'not-self'. Our self-identity, in other words, depends entirely where or how we draw that boundary line.

We come to feel that 'I am this and not that' by drawing a boundary line between 'this' and 'that' and then recognizing our identity with 'this' and our non-identity with 'that'. For example, we may have very clear values concerning cruelty to animals and will draw a distinct boundary between us and others who are seen to cause harm and suffering to animals. Or we may consider our self to be a firm disciple of the discipline of psychology and believe in the study of the individual as the fundamental science. In this way we develop a notion of 'me' and everything I psychologically consider to be 'me' is on the inside of the boundary. Anything I consider to be 'not me' is outside the boundary. In this way we create a psychological boundary between 'me' and 'not me'. An effect is that we now assess 'not mes' by their personal beliefs and actions. In this way we make judgements about others as to their inclusion or exclusion. For example we may consider that those who are from the discipline of psychology will be included in our boundary but others such as psychoanalytically informed social scientists who believe in a social psychology may be outside our boundary.

As will be discussed more fully in Section Three, psychological boundaries are also an important aspect of groups. In much the same way as we define the boundaries of the individual, psychological boundaries also define who belongs to the group and who does not: we move from the me and not me to the us and them. This helps us to understand how the group members distinguish external boundaries, separating members from non-members, and internal boundaries, where the phenom-enon of scapegoating is frequently observed. This acceptance or rejection of group members is related to the development of inner psychological boundaries.

Identification and appreciation of boundaries is helpful because we make meaning out of our experiences, and experience itself is at the boundary between the two worlds – external interaction and internal interpretation. The contact point, at the boundary, is where awareness arises. However, as we might suspect, awareness may not be a straightforward experience. Frequently there may not be a match between our internal pool of knowledge and the external experience. In these circumstances the ambiguity that exists at the boundary between our personal knowledge and that which is being sensed can be a source of anxiety, and then it is the boundaries that matter. When we experience conflict between inner and outer worlds we tend to concentrate our behaviour on the differences, not the similarities. A result is that this makes us feel that the markers of such boundaries are of special value, or sacred, or taboo. Contact is the point where the boundaries of the individual ('me') meet other boundaries, such as those of social systems ('not me'). The boundary is at the location of a relationship where the relationship both separates and connects. Viewing this in contemporary terms, the boundary is at the interface.

In other words when we experience conflict between inner and outer worlds we tend to 'dig our heels in' and stick to our own boundaries. As mentioned earlier, the development of psychological boundaries provides us with a degree of comfort and well-being. When we perceive our boundaries to be under threat we feel the need for self preservation. It is as if there is a threat to our very existence. In the circumstances the interface between me and not me may be an abrasive experience. A problem with boundaries is that they can become fixed structural conceptions that prevent learning. For example, a manager may be trying to implement some form of change in her organization when she is confronted with considerable opposition from those concerned. In the first instant the manager may try to explain and persuade others to take on the change. But if she is unsuccessful she may become concerned and anxious that she is not going to achieve her aims. At this point she may dig her heels in, whereupon the interface between her and those others becomes abrasive. The boundary now becomes fixed and all mutual learning and co-operation may now come to an end.

The concept of personality system boundaries is applicable to a great deal of what has been referred to above. So is reality testing, by which we mean the ability to discern the outside from the inside: external interaction and internal interpretation. Adequate perception and the ability to deal with incoming material by logical thinking requires that we have a well-functioning boundary. When adequate perception becomes impossible, the personality boundary becomes disturbed and thinking becomes more animistic (when dusk falls, tree stubs become menacing figures). From the point of view of personality boundaries, regression means a move in the direction of malfunctioning boundaries, and on the other hand progression means re-establishment and reinforcement of boundaries. We may say that this is the point that our manager referred to above has reached. She no longer has a well functioning boundary and reality has disappeared from her thinking to the extent that she is unable to perceive the views of others. At this point feelings and phantasies may predominate to the extent that the others are now experienced as a stubborn, irrational bunch who dislike her personally and are deliberately trying to cause her harm.

The contact boundary is where one differentiates oneself from others. If we are familiar with the information being perceived it will be matched with our previous knowledge and dealt with according to whether we like it or dislike it. But a problem arises when we experience new input about which we have no previous knowledge: something that we have never experienced before. In this situation, we need to find a means of coping with the problem presented. One way of dealing with this information is to try to understand the unfamiliar, by accepting the unpleasurable situation and working at it. Another way is to link it to some previous category that we think it fits into, while yet another approach is to deny its existence and to filter it out. It will be appreciated that in taking either of the last two options we shall either make a very poor and inappropriate decision or a non-decision.

Another situation that can lead to malfunctioning boundaries can arise where we are experiencing conflicting data. Without the ability to make sense of external data by logical thinking we may become highly anxious, perhaps even unable to think. To understand the process of conflict better we need to understand something more of our internal processes. In the following sub-section I shall explore the effects of conflict starting with relevant processes in childhood.

4. Conflict

As was alluded to above, as part of the process of development, within the boundary of the self, the child achieves an inner organization of 'objects'. These may be people, ideas, events, and values that are organized into a coherent system – usually using categories that are determined by the parents. Here the mind becomes a relatively orderly place and only a limited amount of chaos can be tolerated. In some cases ideas become unacceptable to consciousness if they conflict too much with other ideas. The way that the child deals with ideas that are incompatible is by dispensing with them through what is referred to as repression and other defence mechanisms, which will be more fully explained later in this Section.

These are what might be referred to as primitive responses that occur before the infant has developed a sense of self as an individual. As will become evident later in the book, especially when referring to groups, these early experiences are important concepts. Although they are no longer conscious in adult life, the imaginings and memories of infantile experience, particularly when associated with anxiety, have a profound influence on subsequent mental development and help to determine the character of personal and social relationships, cultural interests, and the way of living – they become part of the boundaried self.

Conflict resolution begins as soon as the infant has some control or restraint imposed upon its behaviour by the parents: in other words, as soon as some semblance of conscience has developed. This is achieved by the taking in of external objects which then form internal mental images that become part of our stock of knowledge.

Through this process a rich world of inner objects or representations of external objects is built up in the mind. Early introjections, since they are virtually all the infant has, are particularly potent, and the inner 'objects' they create are never forgotten. These early introjections, which of necessity are of parents or parental figures, create an inner object commonly referred to as the conscience or technically referred to as the superego.

The introjection of the 'good' parent creates what I shall refer to as the ideal conscience; that is, a sense of ideals and positive morality – a pattern of what to do. And introjection of the 'bad' parent creates what I shall refer to as the persecutory conscience, a sense of guilt and negative morality – of what not to do. Initially, conscience is built up by identifying with; that is, forming and taking in and retaining mental images of parental figures. But this is not a static phenomenon and this same sort of process may occur later in life in exchanges between other authority figures such as school teachers and managers in organizations.

Thus, when we are experiencing conflicting data we may compare the data with that part of our internal pool of knowledge that we refer to as conscience. We will compare the data with our pattern of what to do and what not to do. Our beneath-the-surface process, which is out of our awareness, will determine whether the data matches our ideals and positive morality or whether it makes us feel guilty and of the view that this is something we should not do. Conscience provides us with a means of knowing what to do and what not to do. An example might concern someone working in a finance department who is asked by a friend employed in the company to 'bend the rules' by paying him some expenses without attending the office to sign for them. Taking things at face value we might suggest that the finance department employee should be bound by the company rules governing such procedures. But at a beneath-the-surface level he will also be influenced by his conscience. If he feels strongly that this is something he should not do he may also experience strong feelings of guilt that someone should ask him to do such a thing and disgust that the other person was suggesting such irregular practice. His response to his friend may therefore be much more than a straightforward refusal.

But there is never a universal solution that we can apply to all situations where we experience conflict. By conflict we simply mean that two or more drives are opposed in a living situation. The nature and outcome of the conflict that takes place within the mind between the two sets of antagonistic tendencies results in anxiety. Even as adults we can only tolerate a limited amount of chaos. One way of dealing with ideas that are unacceptable to consciousness is to dispense with them by the same mechanisms developed and used in infancy. These 'defence mechanisms', as they are referred to, will be explored later in this Section.

Mental conflict can be anxiety provoking, but we should not forget that the contact point at the boundary is where awareness arises. In many instances conflict resolution can also have considerable benefits. Resolution of conflict is much more likely to be a compromise rather than a solution. It can often be positive and may lead to adjustment and adaptation and the learning of new skills. For example, a manager may find that he or she is faced with a conflict concerning a need to win a contract and a desire to be fair to their staff. The staff may have recently been working hard and have given their all, but to win the contract the manager must now rely on the staff to work longer hours. The anxiety may be so great that the manager finds a way of resolving the conflict by adopting new working practices or adapting current practices to accommodate the staff needs. In doing so, they may all learn new approaches to the task.

In the following sub-section I refer to attitudes and values that are very much associated with conflict.

5. Attitudes and values

We all make quite basic decisions. For example, about whether something is good or bad, right or wrong. Clearly, this is also informed by our internalized pool of knowledge and feelings. Why and how do we learn what to do and what not to do? What is ethical and moral and what is not? In dealing with these issues we have to decide which conflicting idea we shall accept and what happens to the other idea. The answer to these questions lies in the development of beliefs, attitudes, and values.

Attitudes have been defined as relatively lasting organizations of feelings, beliefs, and behaviour tendencies directed towards specific persons, groups, ideas, or objects. An individual's attitudes are a product of the person's background and various life experiences. Significant people in a person's life – parents, friends, members of social and work groups – strongly influence attitude formation. Our attitudes are made up of our beliefs and feelings towards someone or something. We can't observe attitudes per se, but attitudes serve as a guide to behaviour. The behaviours associated with an attitude can be identified by anyone who observes interaction between people. Attitudes are very important to us because they dictate the way we interact with and treat other people or groups of people.

An example could be someone who may have experienced various friends and family members dying in hospital after suffering considerable pain. These sad experiences and the resulting unbearable thoughts and feelings concerning their loved family and friends may result in a developed attitude that they dislike hospitals. When, at some later time, they are in need of hospital treatment themselves, this attitude may effect their need for treatment. Doctors and others may try to convince the person of the necessity for hospitalization and the silliness of their stance, but they may be ignorant of the reason that this attitude developed in the first place.

When evaluative feelings are attached to personal beliefs, attitudes are formed. An attitude can be a conscious and selective judgement about a person, object, concept, or event. But more importantly, they may also develop from unconscious processes as a result of emotional experiences An attitude provides a mental predisposition to behave with consistency toward its subject. As such, attitudes tend to endure or persist over time. But attitudes can be changed and the changeable character of attitudes is important when we seek to manage performance, reduce conflict among groups, shape a corporate culture, or adopt ethical behaviour. Attitudes can apply to general classes of objects or groups, or to a specific person or idea. We can appreciate, therefore, that attitudes will exert a predictable influence on our behaviour.

Attitudes may become a significant part of an organizational culture. For example, there may develop an attitude that human resources (HR) is a good place to work based on experience over a period of time. For most part this is helpful and valuable to the achievement of organizational aims. However, when change is proposed that affects the structure or working practices of human resources personnel there will be a need to be aware of and take heed of the developed attitude of those concerned. If this is not achieved there may well be considerable emotional resistance to the change process.

Attitudes are not the same as conscience but conscience will undoubtedly affect our attitudes. Where, for example, an individual does not have a strong sense of what is right and wrong, of what to do and what not to do, the attitudes adopted may reflect this. Thus, an individual may develop the attitude that it is all right to steal. Conversely, someone with a good sense of what's right and wrong may develop the reverse attitudes.

An attitude represents the interplay of a person's emotions, cognitions, and behavioural tendencies with regard to something – another person or group, an event, an idea, and so on – in the individual's organizational or social world. For example, where someone, or some group, holds a very strong negative attitude about corruption, they will most likely not wish to conduct business with someone or some group who are considered to be corrupt. Conversely, where someone, or some group, is ambivalent about corruption it will not affect their dealings and relationships with anyone else or any other group, no matter what their reputation and practice is regarding corruption.

Beliefs and attitudes often combine to form all-encompassing ideals called values. A value is established when a belief or concept is enduring and provides a personally preferable mode of conduct. Often a value is the sum total of many attitudes that, when taken together, provide personal commitment and consistency; for example, 'honesty' and 'fairness' are values.

We develop what we might refer to as personal values by organizing a constellation of beliefs concerning preferable modes of conduct or existence. Since values are more general or abstract than attitudes, their influence on behaviour tends to be less direct. Like attitudes, values are learned and may change as a result of societal or organizational experience. We conceive of values as normative propositions, held by individual human beings, of the way that human beings ought to behave. Most importantly they are supported by the internalized sanctions of the conscience and function as:

(a) imperatives in judging how our social world ought to be structured and operated, and
(b) standards for evaluating and rationalizing the propriety of individual and social choices.

This approach emphasizes that values are normative standards by which human beings are influenced in the choice of their actions. The primary function of values is that they serve as determinants and guidelines for decision making and action. Not, I should add, conscious decision-making, but unconscious decisions; these are beneath-the-surface processes. When values are evoked they arouse in us all the emotions associated with the original object, which may be positive or negative. Although, of necessity, values have their origins in the influence of parents or parental figures, this dynamic continues through life with societal influences becoming more influential as time goes by.

Taking the example of 'honesty' as a value held by an individual; if we are to gain a true understanding of what the value means to the individual, we would need to trace it back to its roots. We would need to try to understand what caused the development of this value and why it was included in the internalized pool of knowledge in the manner that it was. A likely scenario might concern an incident or series of incidents in the formative early years of the individual's existence when a significant other, such as the mother, had needed to stress the importance of honesty. At that point the individual may have experienced feelings of guilt, shame, and/or a fear of abandonment by his mother. When at some later stage of his or her life the individual is confronted with 'dishonesty'; when his or her values are directly challenged; he or she will experience all the same emotions as they did in the original situation. This is why values are so influential in our lives.

One of the characteristics of personality listed previously was that concerning the way that the individual adopts forms of behaviour that are psychologically advantageous to the individual under the circumstances imposed on them by their environment. This was the case in the infant world and it is also the case in the adult world. It may not be entirely surprising, though, that many of the value–attitude systems that are shared and transmitted by the members of a society are important to the well-being of the society as well as the individual. The individual acquires such desirable values as a result of the social rewards that come with their assumption and incorporation into specific patterns of overt response. The goal of eliciting favourable responses from others stands side by side with every one of the individual's more immediate and specific goals, and no pattern of behaviour can be completely successful and rewarding unless it serves to achieve both.

It can be appreciated that this will have a considerable impact on the individual's decision-making regarding the social relationships he or she develops. Clearly, an individual whose values include those of honesty and decency is most unlikely to join a criminal gang. In developing work or social relations the individual would be much more likely to build relationships with others who held the same or similar values as their own. Indeed, there is much research evidence to show that we seek out others that we perceive as similar to ourselves to form relationships. However, this may not always be possible, in which case the individual may decide to withdraw from the group or organization that has values contrary to his or her own.

An important notion is the understanding that perhaps the most outstanding and the most continuous of human psychic needs is that for emotional response from other individuals. The term emotional response is used advisedly, since the eliciting of mere behavioural responses may leave this need quite unsatisfied. This need is so universal and so strong that many social scientists have regarded it as instinctive in the sense of being inborn. Whether it actually is so or whether it is a product of conditioning is a problem that may never be solved. What we can say is that individuals are so completely dependent on others during infancy that they cannot survive without eliciting responses from their parents or other carers. There is much good evidence that young infants require a certain amount of emotional response for their well-being. In the highly dependent world of the infant one of the greatest dreads must be that of being left alone or abandoned. These are feelings that stay with us throughout our lives. Indeed, psychoanalysts would stress the fact that babies who aren't loved don't live. Since all individuals go through the experiences of infancy, the question of whether this need is innate or acquired is really an academic one. In either case its presence is universal.

It seems clear that this most basic of human needs can only be provided for by the mother in the earliest days of infancy. It does not require too much thought to realize that the mother thus becomes a highly significant part of the infant's life and that the early experiences are so vital to the infant, who is seeking favourable responses from his mother. It can therefore be seen how the early experiences are such an important and meaningful part of development for all of us.

The conscious mind develops slowly, and in some respects remains always dominated by the unconscious. According to psychoanalytic theory, as long as we live our unconscious makes us interpret much of what happens to us in the light of our earlier experiences. For example, our unconscious, on the basis of how we interpreted to ourselves our early experiences with our parents, causes us to believe either that the world is basically accepting and approving of us or rejecting and disapproving. This extends to our belief that we are good or bad persons; it gives us the feeling that we are or are not competent to deal with life; that we are or are not lovable; even whether we will be rewarded or disappointed. Such far-reaching attitudes are formed on the basis of extremely vague feelings that we nevertheless experienced most strongly at a time when, because our reasoning abilities were as yet undeveloped, we could not yet comprehend the meaning of what was happening to us. And since these attitudes that continue to dominate our experiences originate in our unconscious, we do not know what caused them and why they are so convincing to us.

These sorts of attitudes will affect the personality in various ways that will be far from obvious to those with whom the individual comes into contact. For example, some individuals may be experienced by their manager as infuriatingly lacking in confidence while others may be experienced equally infuriatingly as over-confident. Those lacking in confidence may be full of doom and gloom and unable to see good in anything. Those who are over-confident may be full of energy and recklessness, supporting any new idea with unthinking vigour. For the manager these may be frustrating individuals who, because of previous experience, will be difficult to develop into the sort of employees desired. However, some appreciation of the way that beneath-the-surface values and attitudes are formed will be a valuable starting point.

Values, then, are an important part of our internalized pool of knowledge. When we experience thoughts or sensations that conflict with our values we are likely to be emotionally involved. When we contemplate something that is contrary to our values we may suffer a very strong emotional disturbance. This is such a fundamental part of us that it may actually have an effect on our bodily functioning, which may be evident by facial reddening; perspiration; or a change of pulse rate. It would seem that by some process changes in our bodily function are triggered by our emotions. By way of example, I can recall an occasion at school when the class were all under suspicion of stealing. In these circumstances I found the thought that I might be suspected of dishonesty so unbearable that I became red in the face.

In the next sub-section I briefly refer to the effect of emotions on our beneath-the-surface world. In some ways this is unnecessary because most, if not all, of the dynamic processes that occur beneath the surface have arisen because of emotions that were aroused at the time. By having a sub-section titled emotions I should not wish to detract from the constant need to reflect on the way that emotions shape our experiences.

6. Emotions

This is, of course, true of our values where the functional importance derives primarily from their emotional content. Behaviour that is not in accord with our values elicits responses of fear, anger, or at the very least, dis-approval. This is equally so whether the behaviour is our own or that of others. Thus, where we perform an act contrary to one of our own established values, we will experience considerable emotional disturbance both before and after. In most cases we will have such a reaction even though we know that the act will not entail punishment. This disturbance may diminish with repetitions of the act, but it is so influential that it will reappear with each new situation involving the particular system.

Similarly, other people's acts that are contrary to one of our values will elicit emotional responses even when they do not threaten us in any way. This projective aspect of values will be familiar to anyone who has had to adjust themselves to life in an alien culture. Even when the members of such a society are completely friendly and co-operative, merely observing certain of their behaviour patterns is likely to make the outsider exceedingly uncomfortable. Some examples of situations that might evoke discomfort for British travellers might be societies that eat dogs, horses, or other animals normally considered as pets. Other examples might concern values such as decency or fair play. But we don't need to go to other countries to discover alien parts of society that cause us discomfort. Some parts of our own society may be experienced as equally alien. I have in mind groups such as those that share racist values.

This may provide us with an insight into what we refer to as institutional racism. Where the predominant values of a group, organization, or institution are those of equality, fairness, ethical behaviour, and a commitment to treating all human beings the same way, the overall effect will be a group, organization, or institution that is guided by institutional ethical behaviour. When racism is experienced at any stage by any part of the group, organization, or institution the members will experience strong emotions associated with their revulsion to racism. It will be experienced by organization members as such unbearable thoughts and feelings that it will evoke responses to those concerned. However, where such values are not predominant the reaction to racist behaviour may not evoke a response because it does not evoke any emotional reactions. We may refer to this latter situation as institutional racism.

Clearly, values are deeply affected by emotions, which are also part of our internalized pool of knowledge. But we can also say the same about other beneath-the-surface processes previously referred to, such as classification and conflict. Even the example of dogs, which was a mainly cognitive, surface process, concerned beneath-the-surface dynamics. Almost everything we do is affected by emotions and in those situations where there is a distinct absence of emotions we would be well advised to reflect on what is happening to the emotions. We might well ask what we have done with them, or where they have gone. We shall see as this Section progresses that we devise all sorts of ways of shutting out our unbearable thoughts and feelings. However, we should always remember that at one level they always exist. Experiential learning and emotions may not be as obvious as the other, cognitive type of learning, but they are also ever-present even though all of this is occurring beneath the surface.

Taking things at face value and treating people as if they were rational, logical beings that can be taught to follow systems and procedures may seem an attractive proposition, but this is an illusion. Emotions are ever-present and have an important influence on everything we do. We may not be fully aware of what is occurring beneath the surface but that is not to say that it is not happening. Take, for example, the common experience of driving a car. The less aware you are of how to drive a car, or of the traffic conditions you are driving through, the more tense you are, the more anxiety you will experience, and the firmer hold you will keep on yourself. But, on the other hand, the more experienced you are as a driver and the more conscious you are of the traffic conditions and of what you need to do in emergencies, the more you will be able to relax at the wheel, the less anxiety you will experience, and you will have more of a sense of control. You will have the awareness that it is you who are doing the driving, that it is you in control.

As with any other activity, driving a car is not just an activity; it involves both thinking and feeling. If we were to limit our reflection to thought only, we would ignore a huge part of our experience. Many readers will be familiar with the extreme feelings associated with road rage. How could we possibly say that the activity of driving a car only concerns thought? Clearly it involves varying degrees of feelings, as does all human activity. Faced with any experience, the emotional learning that life has given us, such as the memory of a past disastrous relationship, sends signals that streamline our decision-making process by eliminating some options and highlighting others at the outset. In this way the emotions are involved in reasoning – as is the thinking brain.

If we return to the example concerning dogs it may help us to see the way that emotions are involved in our reasoning. Our original classifications of dogs as 'man's best friend' and 'ferocious beast' didn't just happen. These classifications clearly developed from some sort of experience concerning a dog or dogs. If our experience was one of man's best friend we almost certainly experienced feelings such as love and affection; whereas if our experience was that of ferocious beast we almost certainly experienced feelings such as fear and hatred. When at some future occasion we see a dog these same feelings are evoked and both the object that is dog and the object that is the associated feelings are invoked in our reasoning. The same sort of process will occur over and over again in regard to human objects such as friends, associates, colleagues, and family, whom we will have classified in different ways. For example, our favourite aunt, our best pal, our partner; or our mean uncle, our interfering neighbour, our bullying boss, and our office creep. When we encounter these people, or when they come to mind, they evoke our emotional feelings about them and these are invoked in our reasoning every bit as much as what they are actually doing.

There may be occasions when we may not be able to harmonize our thoughts and emotions. A result may be that the strength of our emotions may disrupt thinking and perception. Emotions may be so overwhelming that they may even prevent us from thinking and perceiving what is happening around us. This state of a lack of perception may come about through any situation where strong emotions are aroused. This could be fear and anxiety, enthusiasm or excitement, or over-involvement or alienation. There are occasions when things may be so bad that even the most able is left in this state of lack of perception. An example might be that of the watch industry, which was suddenly and rapidly confronted with the problem of cheap, battery operated watches. This development changed an entire, long-established industry overnight, and must have been a huge shock to all concerned. Faced with such circumstances I feel sure that in the first instance many concerned would have been left feeling totally helpless, distraught, and as if the end of the world had come; feelings that left them so overwhelmed that they were prevented from thinking or perceiving.

Fear and strong anxiety are obvious examples of situations that may prevent us from thinking. But the same thing can happen in regard to any situation where strong emotions are experienced. The way that strong feelings of excitement can prevent thinking is often revealed in sports matches where a team or individual score a goal or point and are then at their most vulnerable for a short period. In view of our very basic needs for attachment, we should not be at all surprised that strong feelings of alienation would cause us to be so overwhelmed as to be unable to think. Understanding and appreciating the part that emotions play in our everyday lives is an important part of understanding beneath-the-surface activity.

Having an awareness of the beneath-the-surface part that feelings play in our daily activities, including the cognitive aspects, is important. But equally important is the way that we devise all sorts of beneath-the-surface processes to deal with our unbearable thoughts and feelings. The way that individuals react when rational conscious processes fail us; the ways that we find of coping with anxiety; are of particular relevance to an understanding of behaviour influenced by beneath-the-surface processes. It is important to realize that these developed processes also become part of our pool of internalized knowledge and feelings. These processes are too numerous to include in this volume but the more significant of these will be explored in the following sub-sections, starting with repression.

Dealing with unbearable thoughts and feelings

7. Repression

Faced with the anxiety that arises from unbearable thoughts and feelings there are several courses of action that we can take. One of the ways that we learn to cope with really bad news is by shutting it out of our lives completely. By repression, as it is called, we relegate something unbearable to our unconscious. In other words, we exclude these thoughts and feelings so that they no longer have any direct influence on consciousness or on behaviour; the individual then normally becoming quite unaware of the existence of any such tendency within their mind.

Since here, and throughout the book, I refer to the concepts of the unconscious and the subconscious, it may be helpful to discuss their difference. A person is normally unaware of what goes on in either their unconscious or their subconscious. However, through a careful examination of their thoughts, feelings, and motives, the content of the subconscious will usually be accessible to them. The process may be a difficult one, but it is possible for them to bring into awareness what goes on in their subconscious. By contrast, there is a nearly impenetrable barrier between their conscious and unconscious minds. This is because what goes on in their unconscious is what is unacceptable to their conscious mind and has therefore been severely repressed. Full awareness of what goes on in the unconscious can be achieved, if achieved at all, only against the greatest resistance. To penetrate this barrier, or boundary, separating conscious and unconscious, we may need to struggle with the resulting emotions by making a concentrated and determined effort. In many cases this may be possible only to a limited degree, or even quite impossible.

The unconscious mind consists mainly of repressed sentiments that have their foundations in infancy. By repression we mean the exclusion of painful and unpleasant material from consciousness. The sort of thing we are talking about is an experience in childhood that we may perceive as too horrid to bear; for example, a child feeling neglected when a new-born sibling arrives. The feeling of abandonment is so unpleasant that this experience and the feelings associated with it are repressed into the unconscious. A further example might concern a child who experiences the break-up of their parents' marriage, with the father leaving the family home and setting up home with another partner. The child may feel so distraught, angry, and let down that they will repress or blot out these painful and unpleasant feelings from their conscious. It is not difficult to understand, then, that repression is used as a means of defence against unpleasant feelings – a defence mechanism. However, it must also be apparent that it is also an unconscious one, for the subject – like the child referred to above – does not realize that they are repressing certain sentiments.

Being repressed into the unconscious does not mean that the original experiences and their associated emotions are gone for ever. They are still part of our self-concepts, which are the individual's views of himself, so that when at some future time the individual concerned has an experience that, when compared with his pool of knowledge and feelings, is considered similar to a category of experience that has been repressed, he or she will automatically attach to this new experience all of the emotions that were part of the original experience. In this way, when an individual experiences an authority figure seemingly abandoning them or, to take the second example, an authority figure letting him or her down, this part of the pool of internal knowledge is compared with the present experience.

Our self-concepts begin in childhood and expand through object relations, first with the mother and then with other significant family members. The object relations with the parents provide a continual psycho-social basis for learning what is pleasurable and what is distressing. The way that we, as individuals, will respond to any situation will depend greatly on the given situation as we have learned to perceive it. As has been explained above, the unconscious mind contains mental tendencies and traces of past experiences that once acted in full consciousness. These affect our behaviour without entering consciousness; they may also come back into consciousness again, given the appropriate stimulus. Thus, something in our distant past is transferred into the present. By this process a present-day authority figure that is experienced as letting an individual down is, in effect, experienced as the father, and all the emotion associated with father is now present in this experience.

As the infant grows up they soon realize that certain of their actions and, most importantly, their feelings, evoke disapproval in adults, and these forbidden impulses tend to be pushed out of consciousness by this mechanism. For example, it may be the case that it is not acceptable for children to express their anger and they subsequently grow up seemingly placid individuals. Although repressed and unconscious, this does not mean that these feelings are not present, they are simply blotted out. Still being part of us they affect our behaviour in ways we are not aware of. Taking the example further, should this placid individual go to work in a macho organization he or she is likely to be regarded as weak. For the most part this may be true, as he or she will have split off and blotted out the wish to express their feelings of anger. However, the wish is still present and a possible outcome is that the individual referred to may, after some time, 'snap' and become more angry than the average person. This is a further example of the way that our behaviour is frequently influenced by motives and attitudes beneath the surface of which we are quite unaware.

Perhaps a further example will serve to explain this more fully. As part of the process of growing up children will frequently be confronted by objects (human or otherwise) that frighten or scare them. The most likely response is to flee to the protection of mother or father. The response of the parent will range from an attempt to develop understanding of the circumstances, whereby the child may face further such scary moments on his or her own, through to a response that told the child 'not to be silly', in which case the child might have to face further scary moments on his or her own and thus develop a way of coping, which might be to deal with it by denial. From time to time, we will all experience feelings of fear. We may not be aware of it, but our response will be influenced by the way we developed our approach to fear, perhaps many years earlier.

Being a reflective manager will not lead to a means of changing individuals whose attitudes seem unhelpful. Indeed, it is far from my intention that anyone should attempt to do so. However, understanding that an employee who exhibits a lack of bravery or an excess of recklessness is not necessarily a coward or a cowboy, but that somewhere in their past they may have developed these attitudes as a means of coping, may be helpful to both parties.

I should not wish to give the impression that the process of repression only applies to childhood. The essence of repression lies in the function of rejecting and keeping something out of consciousness. Even in adult life, when we experience extreme anxiety the object of the desire involved tends to crumble a little. For example, we may be very ambitious and have a strong desire to gain a promotion at work. We feel we have worked hard and have the necessary qualifications, and think we should have a good chance of success in the pending selection process. In the event, we are not successful, but we put our trust in the fact that a further opportunity will arise within a short while. At this stage, we are able to cope with the anxiety of not achieving our aim.

A problem may arise, though, when we go through a further selection process only to once again find that we are unsuccessful. Now we may experience a different level and quality of anxiety. Faced with the unacceptable idea that we are a failure, extreme anxiety or panic may occur, and if that happens often enough we will find it totally unacceptable to our consciousness. It will be blotted out from our psychological world. In this case, the individual will repress his or her desire for promotion and totally blot it out of his or her consciousness, the desire will be 'collapsed' and forgotten. Repression has been achieved and the object is annulled, psychologically speaking.

Repression, the total exclusion from consciousness of painful and unpleasant experiences, may be seen as the ultimate response, but there are many other defence mechanisms that we use that also provide us with an escape from painful and unpleasant experiences. Some of the most common, unconscious and beneath-the-surface means of coping are explored in the following sub-sections.

8. Defence mechanisms

When we experience fear from the environment we can perhaps avoid it by running away, or getting out of the way, or we might even decide to fight off the source of our fear. However, this is not the case with regard to fears arising from within. We can't run away from these fears and we can't fight them; they are with us wherever we go and whatever we do. They are a part of us. The more difficult the task that we are presented with, the greater the difficulty of making sense of the situation, the more likely it is that we shall find ways of coping that may inevitably include the use of various unconscious defence mechanisms. The sort of approach we adopt will depend upon our experiences of previous situations and, more specifically, all our previous experiences of conditions under which given desires could and could not be satisfied.

Where the conflicting input is regarded as contrary to our personal values, or connects to past emotional experiences, the differences will be even more anxiety provoking. Personal psychological strength is dependent on the repertoire of coping responses the individual has developed and on the ability to withstand frustration, which is dependent on the way the individual has dealt with past crises. We know that some people, as they go through life, get more and more bowed down, burdened by one failure after another. If failure has been our experience in the past, the chances of future failure are greater when we are faced with another difficult situation. Conversely, if we have enjoyed many successes in the past, the chances of succeeding are greater when faced with another difficult situation.

When faced with unbearable pain, anxiety, or threats we find ways of avoiding or reducing the unbearable so that we can continue undisturbed and free of the threats pain or anxiety. There are two stages of anxiety that can be differentiated quantitatively. First, there is a small amount of anxiety, which is the initial signal, the sort of little switch that comes on first. This is called signal anxiety. This is the reaction that occurs at the initial perception of danger, and is a call to fight or flight. In most instances this will be a temporary dysfunction, such as the times when we feel we just need a little time to clear our heads and think things through. However, if our efforts at relief fail and perceived danger continues or increases, and we have no means of adaptation or adjustment that will enable us to cope with it, we are in trouble. When the anxiety increases to a certain threshold we say it changes from signal anxiety to actual anxiety.

At this level, anxiety now becomes not a call to action, but a burden. Instead of being a stimulus to fight or flight, or to adjust in an active way, after it passes a certain threshold it becomes a force that becomes an increasingly regressed mental state where we may adopt an increasing use of fantasy, magic, and irrational methods. This is similar to the example I previously provided regarding the individual who fails a promotion interview. On failing at the first occasion he or she experiences signal anxiety, but on failing at the second occasion he or she experiences actual anxiety: now the thoughts and feelings are unbearable. A similar situation might occur with a Managing Director (MD) of an organization who experiences anxiety when the quarterly financial figures show a considerable loss. At this point signal anxiety may cause the MD to take notice and to agree some sort of strategy that is intended to stop the financial losses. However, when a second quarter's financial figures show a continued and increasing financial haemorrhage, the perceived danger may now increase to such a level that the MD experiences actual anxiety.

Stress, worry, pressure, whatever we choose to call it, is a painful experience and we all try to find ways to soften the impact of this pain. Put another way, we develop ways of coping. Thus, when faced with pressure such as that concerning the MD referred to above, we may typically deny there is a problem, blame someone else or 'bad luck', or we may make use of a whole repertoire of methods of coping. Several are referred to in everyday conversation and will be familiar to the reader. All defences referred to are unconscious psychological processes of thinking and feeling that have the objective of reducing anxiety from stress and conflict among different needs. As with much of our behaviour, defence mechanisms are not to be regarded as good or bad. Above all, they serve a useful and necessary purpose of reducing anxiety.

Throughout our lives we develop a repertoire of coping techniques that we employ in difficult situations. This repertoire of techniques, or ways of handling anxiety, be that anxiety arising from external or internal stimuli, is largely built up from the experience of having faced difficulties, having gone through crises, and having overcome them in novel ways. These ways of coping then become part of our normal repertoire, and of course, the repertoire is added to throughout life. It may be enriched in a negative way, but in any case it is expanded. In the short term, these coping methods do give us relief from the painful experience, but there is a downside, because these activities create blind spots in our thinking. A result is that the problem still exists and may be getting worse because we have not addressed it. At some point, others may see the problem and start to criticize and thus the pressure may build to an intolerable state. This situation can have an adverse effect on the performance of not only the individual but also of those associated with him or her, be that in a family, work, or social capacity.

Rationalization

Perhaps the most familiar type of defence mechanism is that which we refer to as 'rationalization'. I feel sure that every reader will be aware of this form of coping and will be able to reflect on the many occasions that they have used this defence mechanism when faced with anxiety. Put simply, 'rationalization' is the unconscious manipulation of our opinions to evade the recognition of the unpleasant or forbidden. Thus, an individual who was having difficulty coping with their job might claim that they did not know what they were supposed to do. By unconsciously manipulating his or her views the individual is able to avoid the unpleasant experience of not being competent. In this way the individual evades the panic associated with failure. A further example may be a manager who has just seen his company lose an important contract and, instead of living with his painful experiences of frustration and disappointment, he might rationalize the position by saying something like, 'They'd have been difficult to work with anyhow'.

To return to the MD referred to above, let us assume that in childhood he or she may have developed a means of coping as a result of his or her parents' demands when at school. The parents may have been setting high expectations regarding a subject or subjects that the young MD-to-be was not very good at. Because he or she became repeatedly anxious about being confronted by the parents, he or she developed a means of coping that involved telling the parents that he or she was really doing OK, this was just a minor setback, and results would be fine in the future. I would remind the reader that although portrayed rather logically, this process within the

MD would be occurring in an unconscious beneath-the-surface manner. But let me resume our scenario. Now in position as an adult and MD of the company, he is faced with what amounts to financial ruin. Unconsciously comparing his current experience with his pool of internalized knowledge and feelings he locks into his 'successful' way of coping with criticism and failure by again making use of rationalization; telling shareholders and employees that they were really doing OK, this was just a minor setback, and results would be fine in the future. Nearly everyone else in the organization may realize the danger, but the MD is oblivious because of his blind spot created by his developed means of coping.

The fact that we are familiar with these concepts should not hide the fact that, being unconscious psychological processes, they occur beneath the surface. They are unconscious responses and they become an experience because we are the meaning-making context. This example serves to highlight the way that the activity of being a person is the activity of meaning-making. If we as human beings did not take in our various sensations and translate them into something they would not be what they are. It is about the doing that a human is. In the MD example, it is a human experiencing anxiety and responding from his or her unconscious.

Denial

Another defence mechanism that we will all be familiar with is that which we refer to as 'denial'. As the name suggests, denial is the unconscious process of disowning some aspect(s) of a conflict, with the result that the conflict no longer appears to exist. It is to be distinguished from conscious denial, which is a wilful act. Here we are referring to unconscious activity that is occurring beneath the surface. Denial refers to aspects of a situation that the person does not want to perceive. For example, the owners of a failing company may adopt the view that it is not really a problem, that the company is producing a wonderful product and that they are bound to be successful. The fact that no one is buying the product is denied. Or, a further example may concern a parent who, faced with the knowledge that her child is taking drugs, may deal with the problem by saying that her son is a good boy who wouldn't do such a thing.

In both of these instances there is a denial of the external data, which is what many of us may find ourselves doing. Faced with really bad news that we find so unpleasant and so unbearable to our consciousness, we disown it by the unconscious process of denial. But like all unconscious activity the reality is still present in both the external world and in the depths of our unconscious. We may say that denial is a more or less futile attempt to deny the obvious reality. Even though the thought is unbearable and the mother may deny that her son is taking drugs; or that the thought of the company going bust is equally unbearable and those concerned deny that it is failing; the facts remain unchanged: the son is a drug taker and the company is going bust.

Sublimation

A further defence mechanism is that which we refer to as 'sublimation'. This concerns the redirection of unacceptable aspects of the self into areas that are acceptable to others. The term sublimation is used to cover all conflict resolution that leads to satisfactory results for the individual and perhaps his surrounding society and culture. It is the most desirable mechanism, as it is the most constructive. It makes the unacceptable acceptable and useful. An example might be a football manager who may find a long-range solution to his failure to achieve his ambition to lead a successful team by becoming a television or radio pundit. A further example may be a medical student who, on failing his examinations, suffers high anxiety and is faced with unacceptable and unbearable thoughts and feelings of failure. He then sublimates his drive to become a doctor by becoming a physiotherapist. By this process he finds a way of coping with the anxiety in a way that enables him or her to achieve something acceptable to friends, family, and society in general.

In reading about the lives of many great people, it is often possible to assess the effects of sublimation on their careers. It cannot be coincidence that most have achieved success in spite of obstacles as much as because of positive goals, support, and encouragement. Indeed, it appears that a combination of strong frustration and positive encouragement is a part of every great person's biography; that failure to achieve the heights of success in one's original ambitions is sublimated into an even greater ambition to succeed with a new ambition. It seems that the unbearable experience associated with the original failure has the effect of encouraging the individual to do everything possible to avoid the painful experience a second time around.

Regression

Another of the well known and frequently used defence mechanisms is that called 'regression', which may be

51

described as a reversion to a less mature level of behaviour. The basis of regression is that the individual mentally returns to an earlier period of life that was more gratifying or less stressful than their present period. Doubtless many readers will recall occasions when they have been accused, or have accused others, of 'behaving like children' – a sure sign of regression. In its mildest form it is the result of a drop-out of a desire without any replacement by new substitute desires. It's a bit like 'sulking' or 'having a tantrum'. It is rather like a manager who, finding the activity of running a business highly stressful and anxiety provoking, gives up on his or her desires for success and efficiency and decides that the next management meeting will be held on the golf course; he or she no longer treats the business seriously. Rather, it is treated as an object of play. It seems that one of the effects of regression, and for that matter all defence mechanisms, is that it provides a relief from the anxiety to the extent that we can regain our balance on a lower level

Identification

An important defence mechanism is that which we refer to as 'identification', which involves the substitution of one's actual desires by 'existent' external desires. What the person adopts will come closer to what they mean to adopt. An example might concern the identification by a footballer with a star player such as Pele or Ronaldo as a defence against a desire that cannot be, or is not being, satisfied; that is, the desire to earn all the glamour and fame and be admired by many. It will be recalled that one of the greatest dreads of the infant, which continues into adult life, is the fear of being abandoned. Therefore we constantly seek to gain favourable responses from other people. One of the ways we avoided anxiety about abandonment when we were infants was to identify with our mother and significant others. By taking in and adapting to mother and qualities of mother we could be assured of favourable emotional responses.

In adult life we make use of this defence mechanism in a similar manner. For example, being a middle manager in an organization we might have desires to be a senior manager. To avoid the anxiety that we experience around the matter of not being a senior manager we may identify with one or more senior managers and act like them. This identification with qualities of significant others is often evoked when we seek an answer to a problematic and conflicting situation. On comparing the sense data with our pool of internalized knowledge and feelings we may refer to what our old boss would have done and unconsciously act in that manner.

Identification with the aggressor

A particular form of identification is that referred to as 'identification with the aggressor'. To conquer our misery we can identify with the person who appears as a source of danger to our desires. Thus, we can take the word identification as meaning our desire to behave and be like the aggressor, who is thus internalized in our mind. An example might be a manager or leader who is seen as a source of danger because they are perceived as being all powerful and demand submission by bullying and humiliating members of their staff. To conquer the misery of their unbearable thoughts and feelings the workers may identify with the manager or leader and seek relief in 'being like the aggressor'.

53

Identification means that we want to be like the aggressor. Thus, the aggressor that is introjected in the mind is the aggressor with all their severity, their authority, their absolute law, their omnipotence. This introjection now occupies a special place in the mind, constituting what Freud called the superego. One of the results of this sort of defence mechanism is that those identifying with the aggressor take on the characteristics of the aggressor. This is why we see the phenomenon whereby a child who is often and severely punished by their parents will frequently become such a punisher themselves, whether with respect to others or by turning against the self. Thus, abused children may become abusing parents. In the same way, abused workers may become abusing managers and leaders when they take on those roles.

These examples of well-known defence mechanisms referred to above are important because they demonstrate the way that our meaning-making process operates. Faced with an experience which to 'me', a unique individual, is painful and unpleasant, I adopt a form of behaviour that is psychologically advantageous to me. I respond in an unconscious manner by adopting a defence mechanism as a means of coping with my anxiety. It will be appreciated that this is a subjective process and other 'mes' may not have found the same experience unpleasant or painful and were thus able to accept the psychological reality. The important thing is to remember that these developed defence mechanisms or methods of coping become part of our internalized pool of knowledge and feelings and therefore serve to unconsciously guide our decision-making in circumstances that resemble the first occasion when the defence was developed.

Although these and other defence mechanisms have their origins in beneath-the-surface processes of individuals, it will be clear from the examples provided that they may have a considerable impact on all aspects of groups, organizations, and institutions. Without an awareness of these processes we might simply accept the responses at face value and, for example, accept the position that a serious problem is only a minor setback or that there really isn't a problem at all. In other words we may go along with the rationalization or denial. But we will also recall that these processes only serve as a means of escaping from the anxiety arising from the painful experience and the experience still remains. Perhaps of greater importance, these processes are replicated in group behaviour, where they may have an even greater impact on organizations.

In the next sub-section I continue with further examples of the ways that we cope with anxiety. The processes are those that develop in the earliest stages of infancy. These are the primitive mental processes of splitting, introjection, and projection that stay with us throughout our lives.

9. Splitting, projection, and introjection

In the earliest days of our existence the infant is engaged in what is referred to as primitive mental activity. At this stage life is a disorganized world and when, as a child, we are suffering from frustration and anxiety we respond in very primitive ways. When other people interact with the child things are simply experienced by the child as 'good' or 'bad', depending on the perceived experience. This is a 'black and white' world where grey does not exist, and this is the most natural way of dealing with matters at the earliest stages of emotional development. Where other people are experienced as providing satisfaction of desires they are experienced as 'good'; no matter that it is the same person who, at another moment, is perceived as thwarting the satisfaction of desires and is thus experienced as 'bad'. These views of black and white may be arrayed in the primitive manifestations of love and hate. At this stage the infant is simply unable to distinguish other than at the level of black and white.

Considered more closely, the processes of the mind originate in the instincts, drives, or desires seeking satisfaction in objects – frequently in other people. We may thus think of the mind as the apparatus that links desires to their objects, or that mediates between the internal reality of the child and the external reality of objects. Thus, the infant may seek satisfaction from the mother for, say, hunger. On most occasions food in the form of mother's breast will arrive and the infant will be satisfied. However, there are bound to be occasions when the mother is unable to respond and the need will not be satisfied. In this world the infant responds by using primitive defence mechanisms that have been identified and categorized as 'splitting', 'introjection' and 'projection'. Although these are psychoanalytic terms, they may also be described in quite an ordinary way as precisely what the words denote. 'Splitting' means precisely that; splitting of an 'object', be that a person, a value, or a concept, into two different parts that are exclusively identified as 'good' and 'bad'. By 'introjection' we mean the taking in of an object, again be that 'object' another person, such as mother, a quality of another person, such as loving, or a concept, such as trust. And 'projection' is the projecting out, the pushing out from the self of an 'object', such as unwanted aspects and feelings of the self. Thus, the child may push out their feelings of frustration, anger, or inadequacy that they do not want to own.

I need to stress that the mental processes employed at this stage of life are not at all sophisticated. These more primitive desires, or more primitive forms of satisfying given desires, are also more aggressive or destructive. Those who have studied young children have shown that when the child seeks to bring about the permanent removal of a competitor or rival, the ideas of death or murder are uncomplicated by the thoughts, feelings, and sentiments that later come to be associated with them. It is a very simplistic world where murderous thoughts really are murderous thoughts. For the young child the infliction of death, be that real or imaginary, is simply the most natural way of proceeding. This is a world before the infant has developed a conscience; before they have developed notions of what is right and wrong. It is a world before the child can differentiate between what is me and what is not me.

When the child is threatened with loss, either of objects, including human objects, or of satisfaction, or of integrity, the reaction in the mind is anxiety. In common with other behaviour, aggression is an aspect of desires and is the twin brother of anxiety. Anxiety is a state of mind in which more primitive, hence aggressive, desires than usual may prevail. If we act on these primitive desires we may speak of aggression. When the infant is hungry or is fearing abandonment, such is the anxiety that in this as yet unsophisticated world they really do want to destroy the bad object that is mother's breast. Fortunately, as a result of the overall amount of learning that we accumulate through life, aggressiveness of desires decreases with development. Nevertheless, when our desires have not been met and our anxiety builds with increasingly unbearable thoughts and feelings, our aggressive desires may also grow. If they are not acted upon, some form of defence mechanism may become necessary.

The following example may help. Let's say that an employee who is eager to gain promotion and who works hard and skilfully to achieve his aims is constantly thwarted by his manager. The employee, like the infant, may have aggressive, even murderous feelings towards his manager that may even be expressed in terms such as 'I could kill that bastard'. It will be noted that traces of aggression remain; however, unlike the infant, the employee has developed a conscience that serves as a guide as to what is right and what is wrong, and consequently will not contemplate actually killing his manager. His aggression will be limited to language and posturing.

We carry these processes forward into adult life as part of our pool of internalized knowledge and feelings, and in this way they become available through the unconscious processes of meaning-making. Because of their significance in our development, these primitive processes of splitting, introjection, and projection are some of the most important defence mechanisms, and they are frequently found in use in all manner of human settings. These processes, particularly introjection, help us to develop a rich world of inner objects, or representations in our pool of internalized knowledge and feelings. The 'objects' may be of significant people or a quality of another person, starting with our parents, and then other authority figures such as teachers or managers. They may be values and they may be feelings or concepts. In effect, this is the material of our unique individual experience that builds up throughout our lives.

Introjection

Introjection is an unconscious process of taking in all sorts of 'objects'. It will be appreciated that introjections are more than thoughts or ideas. They have their origins in emotional experiences. Consequently, each object, be that a person, value, or concept comes with all the emotional trappings that were present when the original object was admired or feared. Thus, when throughout life good objects are evoked, they arouse in us all the emotions associated with the original object and are seen as promising us all the pleasures and rewards we originally experienced. Conversely, when a bad object is evoked it will arouse in us all the fears, frustrations, and anger associated with the original object. An example of the use of introjection might concern a young girl who, feeling that she is being abandoned, finds that her mother responds by providing her with love and tender care. The good object that is the mother and the qualities of loving and tenderness are then introjected and become objects that are part of her internalized pool of knowledge and feelings.

A result is that when the girl is a young mother she will almost certainly have her own mother as an internal mental image, and this may provide her with support even though her mother may be many miles away. In like manner, a manager may hold, as an internal object, a representation of a past manager from which they may obtain support in the absence of that external manager. In essence what is happening is that when the young mother or manager is experiencing a problem this will evoke a mental image of these people and they will use this past experience to look for support by relating to what they might have done in the current situation. The same thing may apply to circumstances where we may have a perceived enemy to deal with. Here we may obtain support in some sense from an internal enemy; we will recall the mental image of a past enemy and the manner of dealing with them and repeat that behaviour.

Splitting

One of the unavoidable difficulties faced by the young child is the confusion and anxiety of being mothered by a person who provides food and loving but is also sometimes inexplicably absent. The way we, as children, deal with this conflict is by splitting. We split the 'object' that is mother into two parts: a good mother that we love and a bad mother that we hate. In this rather simplistic way we don't have to deal with the more mature concept of someone who can be both 'bad' and 'good'. In adult life we are able to understand that people are psychologically whole individuals who are capable of both good and bad ways of behaving. However, when we are faced with anxiety, particularly extreme anxiety, this may evoke in our unconscious much of our previous primitive experience. In those circumstances we are likely to employ precisely the same device. This sort of beneath-the-surface process is frequently experienced in the workplace. For example, managers who experience anxiety may 'split' their employees into idealized team members who are regarded as 'good objects' who can do no wrong; and others who are denigrated and regarded as 'bad objects', who can do no right.

A further graphic example concerns the leaders of the political party that we support, who are seen as good and admired, while those of the other parties are seen as bad and denigrated. Popular literature also relies heavily on the device of the good hero and the bad villain. The essence of splitting is that a good impulse and object cannot be split off without leaving a bad, and vice versa. Thus, idealization of one object, say the Prime Minister or Republicans, necessarily entails the denigration of another, say the Leader of the Opposition or Democrats – and the greater the idealization the greater the denigration.

Splitting is a very common defence mechanism. It seems that the successful use of this defence as a means of avoiding anxiety stays with us in a very impressive way, so that it is readily available to us when anxiety is aroused. In a family we may deal with anxiety by splitting and viewing mother as a wholly good object and father as a wholly bad object. At school we may view one or more teachers as good objects, who are idealized, while one or more teachers may be seen as the bad objects who are denigrated and detested. In organizations we may view one manager as good and wonderful while another is viewed as bad and unapproachable. I suppose I ought to add that all of us are likely to be the subject of splitting and thus may also be idealized or denigrated. Whichever it may be, it will be appreciated that there is a danger that we become either a little God or a demon.

Projection

Moving now to 'projection', this is the process of attributing one's own unacceptable behaviour to others. A mechanical comparison is that of the film projector: an image inside the object is thrown out on to a screen, where it then appears to have its primary existence. It is the thrusting forth on to the external world, or perhaps more accurately into another person or group, of an individual's unconscious wishes and ideas that would be painful if accepted as part of the self. This may sound complicated, but the following example will help to explain what I mean. Let us assume that we are working in an organization where we are finding it increasingly difficult to be successful. Even our best efforts seem to end in partial failure and our manager is beginning to take notice. We are left with unbearable thoughts and feelings of failure, and unconsciously project these unwanted feelings of failure on to our manager. We no longer own these unbearable feelings and we now see the manager as an incompetent individual who we can blame for our failings.

Some projection occurs in everybody, although usually not with any major dysfunctional consequences. Some common examples of projection are these: the promiscuous housewife who sees all other women as sexually evil and promiscuous; the nefarious businessman who believes that rivals are making every effort to undercut them; the ageing employee who believes that younger employees are jealous of them; the neglecting manager who accuses other managers of neglecting and ignoring team members; the Rovers fan who knows that all United fans are barbarians. In all these examples we can see how painful and unacceptable desires and feelings are transferred to the 'outside world', usually to other people. In precisely the same way we may find that our racist or anti-British views are so unacceptable and scary that instead of owning them we split them off and locate them with the British National Party or the National Front.

Projection, like all defence mechanisms, is an unconscious process that is automatic and involuntary. We may be able to reflect on our experiences at a later time, and we can write about such experiences, but when we are suffering anxiety and use projection as a defence mechanism to cope with that anxiety we are not aware that this is what we are doing. It is a process that was first developed when we were infants and has remained in our internalized pool of knowledge and feelings as a highly influential process ever since. It can be, and is, evoked on frequent occasions, such as during a particularly tense situation at work when the anxiety level may be rising for a number of reasons. For example, a salesman may view the continued interventions of an accounts representative as unhelpful and threatening to a potential contract. Because of this anxiety the salesman may have the painful and unacceptable desire to hit the accounts department representative. This highly aggressive thought is so unpleasant and unbearable that it is unacceptable to the salesman's consciousness. The salesman may project these feelings out and into the accounts representative, whom he may now perceive as being an angry individual who wishes to do the very same thing to himself. Like all defence mechanisms there is a benefit, as this projected desire helps to check the desire within the team member. More precisely speaking, that substitute satisfaction, which is sought in the disguise of another person, seems not only to reduce the intensity of the desire within the salesman to some extent, but also to make it more dangerous to satisfy the desire directly.

Projective identification

A particular and very important form of projection is a process known as 'projective identification', which enables us to understand a wide range of individual, group, and organizational phenomena. Projective identification is both a defence mechanism and an object relationship that occurs in the first year or two of our lives at a stage before a firm differentiation between self and other has been achieved. This is a frequent occurrence between two or more persons, whereby one person projects certain unwanted mental contents on to and into another person with a resulting alteration in the behaviour of the targeted person. It is not just the mechanism of projection, which relates solely to the process of 'getting rid' of unbearable thoughts and feelings by projecting them on to someone else. The difference here is that in projective identification it also affects another person.

To explain further, this important process involves simultaneously a type of psychological defence against unwanted feelings or fantasies, a mode of communication, and a type of human relationship. The unconscious transfer of information that occurs via projective identification is primarily a two-phase process. It begins with the denial and ejection of unwanted feelings that are inherent in a person's unconscious image of a situation. The person therefore alters his uncomfortable experience by imagining that part of it is an attribute of something or someone else, rather than of himself. In the second phase of projective identification, the recipient of the attribution or projection is essentially inducted into the originator's scheme of things. He or she is subtly pressured into thinking, feeling, and behaving in a manner congruent with the feelings or thoughts evacuated by the other.

Perhaps an example from teaching may help to explain the process. A sixth former who is behind on her homework may become very angry because of her failure and is very concerned that she is about to be found out by her teacher. The pupil deals with her unbearable thoughts and feelings by splitting them off and projecting them into her teacher, who at a totally unconscious level is pressured into taking these feelings in and behaving in a way that it is he who is angry and incompetent. The pupil who no longer owns the feelings of anger and incompetence is now able to blame the teacher, who is regarded as having caused the pupil to get behind with her work because of his incompetence. By the use of projective identification the world has been turned on its head.

The example provided concerns a pupil using the teacher to take in and inherit the unwanted feelings. However, we should not be blind to the fact that teachers may also split off their own unwanted feelings and, by projective identification, locate them in a pupil or group of pupils. Doubtless for many teachers feelings of not knowing or incompetence may be hard to bear and unknowing pupils may be a ready source for the location of these feelings.

Projective identification, then, refers to efforts by persons to rid themselves of certain unbearable mental contents by projection and a psychological interaction where the person deposits unwanted feelings into another's feeling system. The first person wishing to get rid of an unwanted feeling treats the other as if they had or embodied the feeling state. A further example may be an individual burdened with intolerable sorrow who may rid themselves of this unbearable feeling and deposit it in others. The others now take in the feelings of sorrow and are viewed by the projector as people who should be pitied. By pitying others he or she may deny his or her own feelings of misery.

The way in which the recipient of this process responds has an important impact on the experience of the sender.

If, as intended by the projector, the recipient simply enacts the role he or she is assigned, then a tacit, collusive agreement is established in which the original meaning of the unwanted feelings or fantasies is reinforced and the defence against thinking about them confirmed. The person who takes on the projections confirms to the projector that he is not like that. Thus, the scapegoat takes on or accentuates the characteristics attributed to him or her and confirms the repugnance the other feels for that disowned aspect. Frequently, the person unconsciously selected as the target of projective identification is someone who is a ready receptacle for such feelings. For example, the schoolchildren referred to above, who may be receptacles for incompetence as they are constantly engaged in a process of learning and are dependent on their teachers.

Where the recipient of the process does not respond by taking in the feelings and enacting the role he or she is assigned; where the targeted recipient does not act on the projections; the projector is left with his or her original feelings. For example, where the pupil who seeks to locate unwanted feelings in her teacher discovers that the teacher does not take in the projections, and does not become an angry and incompetent person, but remains in control and uses his authority to enquire why her work has not been submitted. In these circumstances the pupil has to take back her projections and own her feelings of anger and incompetence.

There is one further defence mechanism that I shall explore in the next sub-section: that which we refer to as 'displacement'. This is a particularly interesting means of coping as we frequently link it with the well known process of scapegoating.

10. Displacement and scapegoating

As its name implies 'displacement' is the substitution of one desire by another, or of one object of satisfaction by another. For example, during a football match a player may become angry because the team is losing and develop a desire to hit the referee. Fortunately for all concerned, instead of carrying out his aggressive wish, when leaving the field the player kicks the changing room door instead. What the player has done is to displace or substitute their desire to hit the referee on to an inanimate object. It may be noted here that although it is a door, the same feelings are associated with this object as were associated with the referee. Displacement refers to an acute impossibility to satisfy one desire and its ready substitution by another. Thus, in this example, the original desire of the player was possibly concerned with success and achievement but, being unsuccessful in satisfying that desire, they became angry and frustrated. The anger and frustration were then located in a desire to hit the referee. These unbearable thoughts and feelings were too painful to consider and as a means of defence against the anxiety experienced this was eventually displaced by an attack on the door.

Put another way, displacement is a shifting of one aspect of a conflict from the original object to a substitute object. In this way the conflict no longer exists in the original focus. Perhaps the most common form of displacement is, as in the example given above, with the affect of hostile aggression that arises from frustration. A manager may be frustrated in a situation over which she has little or no control, such as an unexpected hike in interest rates or a sudden fluctuation in exchange rates. The result may be turmoil and the value of sales may be severely affected in a negative manner. Signal anxiety may change to actual anxiety and this now becomes not a call to action, but a burden. It becomes a force that becomes an increasingly regressed mental state where we may adopt an increasing use of fantasy and magic and irrational methods. This may lead the manager to experience feelings of hostile aggression, initially towards 'them out there', those who have changed the interest rates or exchange rates. However, this may have little effect because 'them out there' are difficult to identify and this only adds to the anger and aggression. A result may be that the increase of the manager's undischarged hostile aggression may then be displaced and directed toward a particular manager or other employee or a group of employees who are then seen as a 'bad' object. This is the familiar and widely used technique that we refer to as scapegoating.

Stereotyping and scapegoating

Stereotypes may be defined as fixed, inflexible notions about an individual or group, and are at the heart of prejudice. They block our ability to think about individuals or groups as the 'other' (the outsider). Thus the usual approach is to concentrate on the 'differences' between 'us' and the 'other'. In doing so we accentuate the way we both behave so that we draw boundaries and then hide behind those boundaries, taking some comfort that there are others not like us and that we are not like them. Having a ready made 'other' to displace our frustrations on to is very convenient. It is all part of the processes occurring beneath the surface.

It may be bad enough that we stereotype all of a certain colour or race as being the same, but it is clearly worse that we attribute to any one of these individuals or groups certain qualities and feelings by way of scapegoating. When we are so concerned and preoccupied with our own uncomfortable and unbearable experiences we look for ways of displacing the unacceptable part of the conflict into some other object. As above, the manager or other employee(s) may be readily identifiable and be seen as an easier target because she will not retaliate. Sadly, we frequently use another individual or group as a means of easing our own distress by the processes of stereotyping and scapegoating.

Perhaps a further example from teaching will be helpful. Parents may be increasingly concerned that their daughter is playing truant and not attending school. When they first become aware of this problem they try to deal with it by reasoning and persuasion, but all efforts end in failure. Now things are beginning to get out of hand and are becoming serious because the school is now pressing to know why the girl is absent and eventually the appropriate authorities are demanding that the child attends school. The parents are frantic and feeling quite helpless, and this eventually turns to hostile aggression. Faced with the conflicting needs of the child and the school; in regard to the child the need to show love and affection and in regard to the school the need to comply with the legal requirements and the need for the child's education, they don't know where to turn. At this point they unconsciously split off their own feelings of hostile aggression and displace them on to the teachers. Now the teachers are seen to be the targets of hostile aggression and not the child. The teachers are being made the scapegoat for the child's truancy.

In this context we might reflect on the need to create boundaries and to make sense out of complexity by categorizing. By the process of categorizing individuals into stereotypes we reduce a complex, complicated, and anxiety-provoking part of our ever changing world into manageable chunks. However, there is a price to pay for this efficiency, because this provides an arbitrary simplicity. By imposing my dichotomous categories on to complex dimensions there is a huge risk of error. There may be a perceptual distortion arising from the sum of categories; i.e., we tend to perceive members of categories as more alike than they really are and we tend to exaggerate the difference between members of different categories.

These distinctive stereotypes can be both positive and negative. For example, all nurses may be seen as 'angels'. At one level we would hope that, being members of a caring profession, all nurses would be kind and sympathetic. However, experience has shown that some nurses may be far from caring and may in fact be harming their patients. There are two potential dangers arising from this type of stereotyping. First, it can create a sort of blind spot, because we do not expect the individual or group to behave in anything but the stereotypical fashion. Second, we place a huge burden on those that we positively stereotype that they will behave in a certain manner. If we take the example of nurses, if they are expected to always be angels what do they do with their anger and displeasure, do they take it home and express it to their family?

This sort of behaviour can be highly disruptive to working relationships and costly in resource terms. Take, for example, the situation where a medical consultant who is visiting patients on a ward is over-burdened with feelings of inadequacy and incompetence regarding a young child he or she may be treating who is not responding to treatment and is going to die. Faced with these unbearable thoughts and feelings the consultant displaces them on to a ward sister or nurse. Not unnaturally, the ward sister or other person 'blamed' will be angry that he or she has been treated in this way. One of the results may be a formal complaint regarding the behaviour of the consultant. From this, a highly bureaucratic system may be instigated that will be costly in time and resources and, regardless of the findings, will very probably leave all parties dissatisfied.

Much of the previous part of this Section has concentrated on negative processes occurring beneath the surface. The next sub-section deals with creativity and provides something of a balance, albeit a limited one.

11. Creativity

As humans we are able to have an awareness of ourselves as separate entities; we have an ability to remember the past, to visualize the future, and to denote objects and acts by symbols; we are able to reason, to conceive and understand the world; and we are able to use our imagination through which we can reach far beyond the range of our senses. Put another way, we are capable of creativity, which has been defined as 'the ability to bring something new into existence'. That something new may take various forms. For example, it may be a new product, a new theory, a new work of art, a new paper or book, a new vision, or a new strategy.

The view taken here is that creativity is not limited to a special class of people – such as artists or writers – or to special products or to special circumstances, as some have argued, rather, that creativity is a drive possessed by all. Whether we are aware of it or not, we all dream and we can all engage in the process of imagination. All of us can and do create 'something new' even if that something new is not an earth-shattering, world-changing creation. In addition, it is suggested that, such is the nature of the drive, we have a compulsion to create. Indeed, we might well ask that if that were not the case, why should I and others continue to write books such as this?

The process of creativity involves imagination, and this may be said to occur in what Freud referred to as the primary process. The primary process method of functioning is well illustrated by dreaming. This is an unconscious process that seems to function as a sort of 'blank sheet'. It seems to avoid the world of internal objects, our pool of internalized knowledge and feelings, and is thus free of all introjections. A result is a purity and originality of thought that produces uncontaminated concepts. New objects are formed that may be said to have a surreal quality. As in day-dreaming it is a means of escaping from the constraints of our known world. That is, a type of mental functioning that is very different from the thought processes that are involved in the secondary process. Here thoughts are very much associated with reality in the shape of comparison of sense data with the individual's pool of internal knowledge.

It has been said that every child at play behaves like a creative writer. That is, the child creates a world of his or her own by rearranging things in a new way that links things of the real world in a way that pleases him. It is this process of linking imagination with the real world that is the process of creativity. It is to be differentiated from phantasy, which is imagination only. This linking takes place in what has been referred to as the transitional space – the potential space between the individual and the environment. The special feature of the potential space is that it depends for its existence on living experiences, not on inherited tendencies. Creative apperception depends upon linking subjective and objective, upon colouring the external world with the warm hues of the imagination.

While we create in the imaginary world of the primary process we exist, and bring our creations into being in the world of reality, which is governed by the secondary process, a world that includes our conscience or superego. Our conscience, which is directed by the superego and instructs us what we may do or not do, is developed from the world of our reality. Consequently, to develop something radically new will almost certainly result in conflict with our conscience, which will be instructing us how we ought to behave. In going beyond the limits set by the world of reality, it may cause us to feel guilty. Guilt is experienced with regard to those others that he or she opposes through his or her discovery, new paradigm, or whatever we choose to call it. Guilt is also experienced in regard to ourselves for daring to 'step out of line'.

Can you imagine the doubts and anxiety that may be present when highly creative scientists develop a totally new concept? For some, the conflict between the new and the existing reality may be so great that the individual will not pursue his or her creation, with the result that it is still-born. The new creation is too unacceptable to consciousness, so unbearable that it is dealt with by denial and blotted out. To be creative requires a good deal of courage, the sort of courage necessary to overcome the inevitable guilt that will be associated with the process. I do not believe that many creative products are formed without

73

the feeling that: 'I am alone'; 'No one has done this before'; 'I have ventured into new territory'; or, 'Perhaps I am foolish or wrong'. A highly appropriate example is that concerning Freud, who, in the face of constant ridicule and threats to his professional reputation, had to have the courage of his own logic. But I have little doubt that he must have given himself some bad frights when he found the key concepts of psychoanalysis arising in his head for the first time.

Seen in the light of a manager, by anticipating future environmental changes he or she can develop adaptive, innovative systems to meet contingencies. He or she can design creative strategies to deal with external affairs. By adopting a creative approach that involves linking the external reality with the warm hues of his or her imagination, he or she is able to create a new response, a new vision, or a new strategy to meet environmental demands. In doing so, he or she will make the team congruent with its current and future environment. However, this process is not without its difficulties, as will be explained below.

Although creativity involves playing, this must not be taken to mean that creative activity is carefree. On the contrary, creative or innovative activity of any kind is invariably associated with considerable violence, and frequently arouses intense experiences of anguish and guilt, as has been described above. A further important aspect of creativity is the turmoil in the internal world of the creative person, which may be something akin to a volcano. Within its depths, the volcano conceals ever-present heat and churning energy, sending out sparks, rocks, and flames at appropriate moments. If prolonged blockage were to occur, however, an explosion would soon follow. If we really believe in our creation we will fight and fight to give it birth and thus bring it into reality.

The view taken here is that violence is an essential element in all creative acts. Such is the intensity of the creative urge that those concerned impose their images on the outside world. Creativity can sometimes be like a volcano that is churning with energy. It screams for release. But if there is no release for that creative drive there will be a tremendous explosion. In an organization this can present a problem, because others may be involved in the adoption and implementation of the creation. Where the creator is a manager who has the power to bring about change and to direct others to carry out his orders, this may present some interesting dynamics. For all sorts of reasons the manager may, in seeking to bring his new creation into being, use coercion and violence to achieve his ends. Experience in various work settings has provided ample support for this view and sheds light on an aspect of 'bullying' that has not previously been given enough attention.

Through the process of creativity, the individual is giving up an external definition of 'reality' and substituting his own, he is therefore giving up elements of certainty and security and substituting uncertainty and insecurity. It is argued that this is one of the necessary risks and costs that we all face when we are creating change. Social change inescapably starts with the individual.

Even though creativity originates in the individual it is still reliant upon other individuals in society for its very birth and survival. If we are interested in groups, organizations, and institutions providing a meaningful, satisfying experience for its members; if we are interested in encouraging members of groups, organizations, and institutions to constantly develop products and processes that are innovative and creative; we need to ensure that the environmental conditions exist whereby the creations of all organizational members, no matter how big or small, are brought into existence; that all organizational members will feel free to explore their creativity in an atmosphere that is accepting and receptive to new ideas. In this way we can help those members of the organization to conquer their feelings of guilt to the benefit of all.

12. Towards relationships

Many of the beneath-the-surface processes described in this Section have concerned relationships, and relatedness has been a constant consideration. In Section Two I explore the way that relational phenomena add to individual dynamics to have an additional impact on group, organization, and institutional dynamics. In this Section the view is taken that when we enter into relationships with another individual or group, further beneath-the-surface phenomena are evoked that, unless they are exposed and understood, may create the unhelpful formation of firm boundaries that prevent progression.

SECTION TWO

Relationships

As ever, the way we choose to view relationships will greatly depend upon the approach that we take. If we take a non-reflective approach each of the parties is likely to come with a label, perhaps a uniform – if not actual, then in the mind – and with all the expectations of that role. For example, we may see relationships as between a manager and a staff member; between a representative of sales and a representative of finance; between a doctor and a patient; between a police officer and a criminal; or whatever. What this approach fails to consider is that relationships take place between human beings. The sort of human beings that were referred to in the last Section; the sort of human beings that have a pool of internalized knowledge and feelings that they unconsciously compare with sense data to make meaning; or the sort of human beings that develop the use of beneath-the-surface processes to enable them to make sense of their world and those that they use to help them deal with unbearable thoughts and feelings.

We should now be more aware of the significant part that emotions will play in all relationships between human beings. For example, at two extremes, relationships can be experienced as harmonious and mutually beneficial, or they can be experienced as acrimonious and harmful. Having developed our understanding from the preceding Section it will be appreciated that in either extreme circumstance strong emotions may be evoked, and this in turn should raise our awareness that beneath-the-surface processes may be occurring. Indeed, we should be aware that some level of emotion and some beneath-the-surface activity will occur in regard to all relationships.

We will also be aware that all beneath-the-surface processes exposed and explored in the previous Section may also be evoked as part of our unconscious process of making meaning of the data presented to us in our various relationships. It might even be the case that before the relationship has progressed to a face-to-face situation, relatedness, the way that feelings and phantasies affect a relationship, may already have set the course for the way the relationship will develop. Bearing in mind that we are constantly in a system of relatedness to others, we will be entering into a relationship with another individual or group, influenced by the various groups to which we are related. And, of course, so will the other party to the relationship.

This Section will concentrate on the way that dynamic processes occurring beneath the surface can have a major influence on relationships. Neither of the parties to a relationship can or should take the other at face value. One or other, or both parties to the relationship may be influenced by political processes; issues to do with power and authority; phantasy relationships; or lack of trust in the other party; all of which are occurring beneath the surface and are not readily available through the usual perceptive processes. In addition, we need to expose and explore what I shall refer to as relational concepts. Relationship is not internal to the individual; for example, we cannot be prejudiced unless there is someone to be prejudiced about. Much of what goes on beneath the surface cannot be viewed solely in the context of the individual. Many feelings and other experiences that we locate in the individual have their roots in relationships. Or they may be affected by the mutual influence of relatedness.

1. Introduction

When people are developing relationships they are
frequently trying to understand the other parties' behaviour and are constantly making interpretations of that
behaviour. Indeed, the ability to make such interpretations reasonably accurately is a necessary social skill. Yet,
this constantly practised skill can be exceedingly difficult
because every direct and immediate experience of feeling
and desiring is spontaneous and unique. That is to say, the
desiring and feeling are uniquely part of that particular
situation at that particular time and place.

Some further problems are associated with different
classifications of knowledge. The type of knowledge that
we refer to as 'knowing about', or cognitive knowledge,
can be communicated through words and symbols that
may be understood in the same way. In many instances,
this type of knowledge will not present too much difficulty in developing relationships. However, where, for
example, different disciplines are concerned, there may be
considerable difficulty as language and words may have
multiple meanings. This may create a circumstance where
mental boundaries impeach knowledge or act to appre-
hend the whole reality, cutting it all the time into little
pieces through perception and language.

But the much deeper and more difficult problems are
likely to occur in regard to the type of knowledge we refer
to as 'knowledge of acquaintance'. This type of knowledge
is a prerequisite to knowing more about the roles and relationships that we are involved in – and this type of learning starts with oneself. This will include our developed
attitudes, beliefs, and values, our conscience, which will
influence our decisions about what we should and should

not do, and all other objects that comprise our pool of internal knowledge. Here we may create emotional boundaries that on many occasions make it impossible to reach or feel each other in our object relations or even ourselves.

If the individuals concerned are not aware of what is occurring beneath the surface, they may be so preoccupied by their own defences, unconscious processes, attitudes, values, and feelings – especially negative feelings such as cynicism; or by their own reactions to the others that these considerations will overshadow the relationship and distort their perceptions and reactions. As has been said, we need to be constantly aware that, faced with any experience, the emotional learning that life has given us, such as the memory of a past disastrous relationship, sends signals that streamline our decision-making process by eliminating some options and highlighting others at the outset. In this way the emotions will be involved in reasoning and relationships – as is the thinking brain.

At the start of the preceding Section it was pointed out that while we need to understand our individual processes of meaning-making, there is never just an individual, we are constantly linked to others through the process of relatedness. In like manner, relationship is not internal to the single person. Indeed, it would be nonsense to talk about 'dependency', or 'aggression', or 'prejudice', and so on as an individual activity. We cannot be dependent unless there is someone to be dependent on; we cannot be aggressive unless there is someone to be aggressive with; and, we cannot be prejudiced unless there is someone to be prejudiced about. All such words have their roots in what happens between persons, not in something-or-other inside a person.

81

This immediately increases the complexity, as we now have to consider not just the self but at least two selves. Learning about the dynamics of life is a matter that has to be considered in the context of a relationship between two people, or two groups of people. For each party to the relationship there is a 'me' and a 'not me', and that will inevitably mean that feelings and phantasies of the 'not me' are likely to be evoked. In the process of developing a relationship, the 'me' and the 'not me' will be connected by the task or purpose of the role that each party is taking up or that they have been attributed in that relationship. In addition, as will be explained below, they may also be affected by roles in other political systems beyond the immediate relationship.

In Section One the concentration was almost exclusively on the individual and on gaining an understanding of 'me'. At various points I referred to the notion of distinguishing between 'me' and 'not me' and at the start of the Section reference was made to the important notion of relatedness. In this Section relatedness is still a vital notion when the focus shifts to an exposure and exploration of the processes that occur in working across the boundary between 'me' and 'not me'; and this is where we start in the next sub-section with systems of political relationships and relatedness.

2. Politics

Be it a family, business, or international diplomacy that we are referring to, in any relationship both parties will be involved in a system of political relationships and relatedness. They are each connected by their own pool of internal knowledge of roles in other political systems. For example, one level of political system within which the parties may perceive themselves to be related is as a miniature element in a set of international relationships. For example, any relationship between an Englishman and an Irishman will very likely be affected by the baggage that each carries as a result of international relationships developed over previous centuries. In like manner, relationships between Americans and Chinese will probably be affected by different lifestyles and cultures. The political system at the international level will be shaped by history and by national cultures and politics, and these are bound to have some effect on individual or group relationships in which they are involved.

Relatedness at the international political system level

A classical example of relatedness at the level of the international political system concerns an Irishman who lived and worked in England, but later returned to live and work in Ireland. In England, to his great dismay, he found that work colleagues were attributing to him the stereotypical views of Irish Republican terrorism. Not in the sense of accusing him of being a terrorist but rather as a 'knowing' associate of terrorists. This left him feeling very despondent, confused, and misunderstood. To make matters even worse, when he returned to work in Ireland he was seen as a 'Brit', and colleagues now attributed to him the stereotypical Irish views of British as oppressive invaders. Needless to say, both experiences were so unpleasant that they seriously impaired relationships.

Relatedness at the inter-institutional political system level

Another level of political system is the inter-institutional political system. In families, we frequently see the inter-institutional political level operating between different parts of the family. This may be especially so between the parents of the respective partners in a marriage. Indeed, we will all be familiar with 'mother-in-law' jokes. They are not part of the particular family but are associated through marital links. Also at this level the political system of a business relationship will be shaped by, among other things, the size of each of the respective organizations; whether they are newly formed or long-established; whether they are cash rich or short of funds; and the organizational cultures. Relating to the other organization may mobilize the individual in, for example, an anti multi-national role and this may evoke a considerable range of feelings. Again, all these factors will have an affect on individual and group relationships that arise out of doing business. They will operate beneath the surface and influence individual relationships.

A typical example of relatedness at the level of the inter-institutional political system concerns a merger of two work units from different organizations. In brief, a Section in one hospital had to close and be located in two other hospitals, the staff and other resources being transferred accordingly. Needless to say, there were considerable practical and logistical arrangements that needed to be considered. But, more importantly, there were emotional issues that concerned the feelings that staff had about the respective organizations to which they were to move. One hospital had a long history of being a leading research establishment and was viewed as an attractive place to work. The other was regarded as 'just another hospital' and not viewed as an attractive place to work. In the circumstances, these emotional issues created considerable difficulties in trying to reach an agreement: in many instances overriding seemingly logical discussion.

Relatedness at the intra-institutional political system level

A further level is the intra-institutional political system. Applied to organizations there will frequently be ongoing disputes between one part of the organization and another. For example, marketing may see human resources as bureaucratic and unhelpful. Should that be the case, then any relationship between representatives of these departments is likely to be affected by the inter-group political system, even though it is operating beneath the surface. Each may be attributed the role of the stereotype attached to his or her department. We all use constructs like this all the time as a way of imposing order and meaning on the world we perceive around us. Also operating at this level are the political systems of one or more academic disciplines, each with its single-minded devotion to the advancement of knowledge – and also its lively competition for publication, prestige, and professional appointments.

In developing cross-disciplinary boundaries there are likely to be many beneath-the-surface difficulties. We may conceptualize other nationalities, organizations, and parts of organizations such as other disciplines based on generalities. By categorizing them into stereotypes we

reduce our complicated world into manageable chunks.
But the price we pay for this simplicity is perceptual distortion that tends to perceive individuals as being
more alike than they really are and then tend to exaggerate the difference. A frequent result is the formation of
rigid boundaries and an interface that is experienced as
abrasive.

For each of the parties to the relationship, much of the
influence at each of the levels described above is similar to
the language that we use; that is, 'part of our taken for
granted assumptions'. As such, each in their own way is
acting in accordance with their unconscious perception of
this situation and may be convinced that they are right.
As an observer of this interaction, or by reflection, we
might consider this sort of behaviour to be ridiculous. But
we need to appreciate that if there is a truth it's in the
person, in each person. You can't come down on one
person with some other person's truth. At all levels of
political interaction there is the potentiality for disaster
and if there is a lack of trust between the parties this
potentiality will almost certainly be realized. It does not
require too much imagination to realize that the greater
the difference between the parties, the greater the potential for conflict and disaster.

Each of the levels of political activity referred to above
are important, but there is another level – the interpersonal level. It is this particular level of political
activity, that which has become known as the 'politics
of identity', that which is a constant element of our
lives, that I shall shortly concentrate on. Before doing
so, in the next sub-Section I take a further look at boundaries with a particular concentration on personality
boundaries.

3. Boundaries – 'me' and 'not me'

Holding in the mother's womb, then holding in the mother's arms, is the first boundary within which the infant's personality can develop. The mother's sensitivity to this growth provides the protection of a boundary that helps the child to extend and expand, and within which he or she can include more and more experience of the world. From the outset this is a two-way relationship; the infant signifies his or her need through crying and gestures. In the beginning, the needs of the infant are very few but are terrifying if they are not met. The degree of frustration that the new-born child can tolerate without disintegrating, without going back to what seems a state of chaos and distress, is minimal.

Here the mother and child are both parts of a dyad: a pair of individuals who function as a unit as a result of their intimate closeness. The infant does not experience the mother as being separate and distinct but rather as part of him or herself. The infant is part of what we will term a symbiotic relationship with the mother, that is, he or she is both held by the mother and is part of the maternal holding environment. A relationship grows through the ability of both parties to experience and adjust to each other's natures. The relationship develops through the infant getting to know the mother as she presents herself to interpret and meet his or her needs, which are emotional as well as physical. The baby needs to have not only food and comfort but also the security of a loving relationship in which he or she can grow and learn to know him or her self and a range of feelings.

The meeting of instinctual needs within the infant with an external object, that is, aspects of the mother's care, not only results in a physically satisfying experience, an interest in the external world, and a rudimentary social relationship to mother, but also initiates the beginning of mental development in the infant. In this way the external world is brought within the infant's grasp. As the infant grows there then develops the use of transitional objects that lead to the recognition of external objects – of a 'me' and a 'not me'. At this stage the polarization of symbiosis – individuation – finally breaks through on the side of individuation, leading to the dissolution of the dyad and the formation of self-concepts. This psychological change arises once the infant is able to experience the mother and other significant objects as separate.

In order to value experience with people in the outside world the child has to gradually make some distinction between what comes from outside and what he or she has the illusion of belonging to him or her because he or she desires it to be so. The second significant stage in the infant's learning about life is the time when he or she realizes that he or she is not the same as the mother who is holding and comforting and making him or her feel happy. This realization is difficult for the child to accept, but by the middle of the first year his or her horizons are expanding. Just as he or she begins to realize that his or her mother is a complete and separate person he or she begins to be aware of father and others who are also separate and distinct.

If the relationship with his or her mother is good enough the infant is able to return to this for strength and relaxation. It provides the child with the continuity of being both in the external world and in his or her mind. Through this he or she is able to cope with these dramatic changes in his or her life. The infant's dependence on this sort of containment by mother will eventually be replaced by the containment offered by the sense of his or her own mind. Development comes about through repeated opportunities for taking in the experience of being held together by someone else and being held in the mind. Through the contact with the mother's capacity for containment of mental states and their transformation into thought, the basis is laid for the development of these same capacities within the infant, by means of internalization and identification.

At around seven months there is a further developmental shift whereby the infant becomes able to experience him or herself and his mother as whole persons. The dawn of the object world is the consequence of the infant's gradual emergence from embeddedness. By differentiating itself from the world and the world from it, the infant brings into being that which is independent of its own sensing and movement. A child's capacity to take his or her impulses and perceptions as an object of his or her meaning-making brings into being a new subject–object relation that creates a more endurable self; a self that does its own praising, so to speak, but needs the information that it is correct as confirmation; a self which can store memories, feelings and perceptions. It is not just the physical world that is being conserved but internal experience also. As well as the emergence of a self-concept, there comes a more or less consistent notion of me.

The infant's journey from dependency to separation and individuation is somewhat of a struggle. Each step towards psychological independence is welcome for the sense of freedom and mastery that it affords. But at the same time the infant is fearful of the threats of abandonment, isolation, and loss of object love. It would appear that the infant is involved in a series of repeated separations from and reunions with the mother in order to overcome the anxiety. In normal development this results in the formation of relatively enduring concepts of self and others. Building from that position the infant is now able to identify the boundaries of self – what is self and what is not self. Without the mother providing the protection of the boundary the child would, at this stage, fail to develop adequately.

It should be stressed that the infant does not go from a state of absolute dependence to absolute independence – independence is never absolute for any of us. The healthy individual does not become isolated but continues to be related to the environment in such a way that the individual and the environment can be said to be interdependent. Even in adult life we dare not give up our unborn need for maternal gratification. We are never completely integrated no matter how healthy we may feel. The evolutionary drive for increasing integration, for improving our capabilities and capacities, brings about growth and development: and this is the principle task for a living being. But integration on any level is never total or perfect: and death – final disintegration – is always present.

As stated in Section One, when we think about 'self' we draw a boundary line between what is 'me' and what is 'not me'. When we answer the question 'Who am I?', we simply describe what's on the inside of that line. Once the general boundary lines have been drawn, the answers to that question may become very complex or they may remain most simple and unarticulated. But any possible answer depends on first drawing the boundary line. In this context it may be recalled that personality is characterized and evidenced by sameness and continuity but is at the same time a dynamic process. Consequently, this boundary line can and frequently does shift. Personalities are dynamic continuums: they can be re-drawn.

Such is our current understanding of 'person' that we have to strain to recover the process in the words 'human being'; we talk about a 'being' and 'beings' as if they were objects. By taking things at face value we may be willing to accept readily presented explanations while ignoring what may be happening beneath the surface. Contrary to normal usage, in this book we are concerned about human being as an activity: not about the doing that a human does; but about the doing that a human is. A central conviction is that personality development occurs in the context of interactions between the organism and the environment, rather than through the internal processes of maturation alone. This is reflected in the psycho-social approach and involves the bringing together of thought and emotion, of past and present, and of psychological and social.

We will recall that the significance of the processes of development that occur while we are in infancy lies in the fact that many of these processes are repeated in adult life, especially when we experience anxiety. Relationships will from time to time almost certainly evoke feelings regarding our original relationship with mother, and we may therefore act in similar ways and use the same processes that we did when infants. In a relationship we will want to be psychologically independent and to feel the freedom and mastery that this offers, but at the same time we may be fearful of being abandoned by the other party to the relationship. Thus, the relationship may involve several separations and reunions as a means of overcoming anxiety.

91

In developing a relationship there will undoubtedly be ambiguity at the boundary, which can be a source of anxiety. Contact is at the point where the boundaries of the individual ('me') meet other boundaries, such as those of another individual or of social systems ('not me'). In highly difficult circumstances there may be what I shall term a 'double boundary'. By this I mean a clear and firm boundary around each individual, the sort of circumstance where neither party is intending to budge from their own respective position. In all instances their position may be influenced by many different factors, some overt and above the surface and some covert and originating from beneath the surface.

The boundary is at the location of a relationship where the relationship both separates and connects. In contemporary terms the boundary is at the interface. If we are to develop a true relationship it is important to see these states as momentary points in a dynamic process, not as fixed structural conceptions. The contact point, at the boundary, is where awareness arises. With awareness the individual can mobilize energy so that the environment can be contacted to meet a need. The danger is that if we concentrate our behaviour on the differences, not the similarities, this makes the boundaries seem like barriers. The truth is that there are likely to be many, many differences.

The situation becomes more complicated when we recall that relationship is not internal to the single person. And as stated earlier, it would be nonsense to talk about 'dependency', or 'aggression', or 'pride', and so on, in terms of an individual. All such words have their roots in what happens between persons, not in something-or-other inside a person. They are related by mutual influence, so that if you want to talk about, for example, 'pride', you must talk about two persons or two groups and what happens between them. For example, where a manager is admired by a worker; the worker's admiration is conditional and may turn to contempt, and so on. You can then define a particular species of pride by reference to a particular pattern of interaction. The same is true of dependency, courage, passivity, aggression, fatalism, and the like. All derive from patterns of interchange – from mutual influence.

The boundary that is a location of a relationship where the relationship both separates and connects may result from the notion of taking up a role. We might describe roles as being claimed labels from behind which people present themselves to others. Roles are also imputed labels, towards which, and partially in terms of which, people likewise conceive, gauge, and judge others' past, current, and projected actions. As soon as we take on a role we draw a boundary around that role, which is regarded as me. In addition, we may also draw a boundary around people in other roles and use them to distinguish what is not me.

A danger is that we are inclined to exaggerate the differences, and this can lead to polarization whereby my perception is seen as right and that of others is wrong. This may be particularly relevant where our field of study is human behaviour. Here we might helpfully consider the role of the researcher. The dimensions of what is and what is not researched and observed are set by the researcher. What those concerned are sometimes not aware of is our own bias that our own unique meaning-making process brings to the situation. Perhaps a good example is my own actions in the Preface where, in taking the role of a psychoanalytically informed researcher, I sought to distinguish and to criticize other social scientists who took up different roles.

It may be helpful to begin to think of the two people to the interaction in a relationship as two eyes, each giving a monocular view of what goes on and together giving a binocular view in depth. This double view is the relationship. Binocular vision gives the possibility of a new order of information and the creation of a boundary around what can now rightly be called a relationship. However, for those reasons already stated – and many other reasons that will follow – the process of developing a binocular view may be fraught with difficulty.

This sub-section will have helped us to gain an understanding of the nature of personality boundaries and in many ways this will be helpful preparation for exploration, in the following subsection, of the remaining level of political activity – the interpersonal level.

4. The politics of identity

This interpersonal level of political activity is possibly the most important notion in developing an understanding of relationships. It is this particular level of political activity, which has become known as the 'politics of identity', that I will now concentrate on. It is so important because it is a constant element of our lives and it affects nearly everything we do. Developing a sufficient level of understanding will inevitably require an analysis of the conscious and unconscious processes through which the biological condition of individuality gets transformed into consciousness of individuality.

This level of political activity has particular implications for individuals involved in relationships. In particular we might consider that every relationship between two individuals is a constant psychological negotiation in which each is trying to impose on the other his picture of the other and correspondingly also to ensure that the other's picture of him fits, or is the same as, his picture of himself. That is the politics of identity. When there is a goodness of fit between the two sets of pictures it produces a sense of stability and security. However, from our previous exploration we will appreciate that this process is naturally complicated by unrecognized and unconscious processes that may contradict what we overtly say and believe. It will inevitably depend upon the way each perceives the other and the thoughts and feelings that are evoked about them.

By way of example we may recall that near the start of the previous Section an example was provided whereby a middle manager developed phantasies and feelings that his female senior manager did not like him. Because he had not received feedback about a report, he had developed feelings of abandonment and this, in turn, evoked in him the phantasy that the senior manager had disliked the report he had submitted. A result was that the middle manager stayed away from the senior manager and had as little contact as possible. As can be appreciated, this may have been very confusing for the senior manager, who had a high regard and liking for the middle manager. The beneath-the-surface processes were totally out of the senior manager's knowledge and awareness.

Sameness and difference

A probable difficulty can be identified at the outset. Going back to that early experience of being separated from mother which brought with it the splitting and projection that results in mother being experienced as 'good' or 'bad', but never both good and bad, we seem to be preoccupied with difference. And, as we know, we have a strong proclivity to turn difference into polarization. From our earliest experiences we learn that there is no me without an other. But more than that, there is no 'me' without the existence of a 'not me' that may well have good or bad values attached to 'not me'. If I wish to feel good about myself on any dimension, it is helpful if the not me is seen as bad.

We need to be aware that there can be no sameness unless there is also a difference. There can be no inclusion without exclusion – and in this context we might consider how we make free use of that word 'we', which can in different contexts be interpreted as including or as excluding. It's sometimes uncomfortable to recognize that I am 'not me' for the 'other'. The 'not me', of course, is not necessarily bad; it can also be good. If, for example, as a middle manager we wish to be seen by our senior manager as a highly competent, serious-minded and capable manager, we may adopt an approach that means we rigorously apply ourselves to the purposes of the organization and never 'slide off' to the pub or a bar for a liquid lunch. We regard 'me' as sober, honest, and reliable, but in order to bolster this view we need to identify the 'not me'. These may be the other managers that we regard as drinkers, those who continually go to a pub or bar at lunch-time: these unreliable and untrustworthy managers that have all the bad qualities that distinguish 'me' as being good.

Polarization is not the only proclivity we carry forward from our early relation with mother: there is also the complementary of the pair, and this applies not only to the sexual pair: for example, we talk of 'bosom friends', each feeling incomplete without the other. In these circumstances we might expect an understanding or co-operative relationship. However, in other circumstances the relationship might not be equal and there might be little complementarity. In other instances there may be a lack of complementarity because it may be a dependent relationship, such as, for example, in the case of a doctor and patient.

The desire for pairing first developed in the relationship with mother and the need for attachment and social approval, is a generally positive dynamic that will be helpful in developing relationships. In some professional circumstances, such as the doctor and patient relationship, we may have little choice. In other circumstances, such as those with solicitors or estate agents, we may have a great deal of choice. But there are many instances, especially in organizations and institutions, when we may need to develop relationships with whoever is deputed by others. In these circumstances, where both different individuals and different groups are faced with the same task, they will share an interest in working together. Here the need for attachment may come to the fore when the task is particularly difficult and anxiety levels are rising.

Me as I see me and me as others see me

One of the interesting results of the process of meaning-making is that for each party to the relationship there may be two versions of 'me' and 'not me'. These may be categorized as me as I see me and me as others see me. The me as I see me will be determined by one's own pool of knowledge and feelings. The me as others see me will be

97

determined by the other's own pool of internalized knowledge and feelings. Suffice to say that these two versions of me may be very different. Where this is so there are most likely to be problems of communicating with each other and expectations of either or both may not be met or may be working against each other. In which case there may be a breakdown in the relationship.

No matter that our intentions may be positive and that we are truly intent on developing a good relationship with another party that is only one part of the relationship: me as I see me. If we are to take a binocular view, we need to consider that the other party may have a very different view. He or she may, for example, view us as someone who is going to be difficult to deal with and not interested in developing a good relationship at any price. That is 'me as others see me'. These two views of self are ever present. If we return to the levels of political activity referred to above and look at the examples given: 'me' may be both an ordinary member of the company and any of the following: 'that Irish fellow, stereotypically a drunk'; or, 'that fellow from such and such a company, stereotypically dominant'; or, 'that fellow from human resources, stereotypically a control freak'. Regardless of our views and our intentions 'me as I see me' and 'me as others see me' may be very different views of this same 'me'.

In any relationship, there is always the possibility that there may be discrepancies in our overt 'external' knowledge of the other party. For example, we may both be going to a meeting knowing that if one is successful in obtaining a larger budget for his or her department the other will suffer a smaller budget. Where that is the case both parties are aware of the circumstances and can relate in a mature and co-operative manner. However, where there are discrepancies beneath the surface, emanating from our 'internal' knowledge, it is most unlikely that the other party will be aware of this. For example, one party may be guided by values that prohibit anything remotely illegal. Unaware of this the other party may try to 'bend the rules' to reach an accommodation. Faced with a rejection of any attempt to 'bend the rules' he or she may simply view the other party as intransigent, awkward, and unwilling to develop the relationship. In reality, he or she is simply doing what all of us do – making meaning out of our experiences.

It may be the case that for both parties to the relationship, there is no match between internal and external knowledge – no real understanding of the other party's position. Coming from what may be seen as totally different disciplines or backgrounds, each has developed internal knowledge quite different from the other. For example, each may be guided by totally different values. We frequently talk of 'common sense', as if meaning is common to a large proportion of society. There may, of course, be some very general notions, such as night and day or men and women, which are common sense. However, once we go beyond the generalization of men and women we may discover that common sense goes out of the window. Such are the influences on each of us that we are unique individuals and consequently we all make unique meaning of our experiences.

If we were to go down the road of common sense we might well end up stereotyping all women or all men. If our meaning-making has resulted in a stereotype of males as unfaithful and untrustworthy, we may consider all males in this way. If our meaning-making has resulted in a stereotype of women as carers, we may consider all women in this way. Seen in print this seems a ludicrous suggestion, but we will be aware that processes occurring below the surface may well bring about such a situation. These examples may appear bad enough, but when we extend our meaning-making to include members of ethnic minorities, other religious groups, and other nationalities, splitting and stereotyping may bring about some ghastly results.

If, for example, we employ the primitive defence of splitting to enable us to deal with someone of another, different nationality, we may see them as wholly bad and incapable of good. We see them in black and white terms. In this world there is no grey, no possibility of being capable of both good and bad. If, because of our own anxiety in dealing with this other of different nationality, we project into them our own feelings of anger and other primitive feelings, there is every chance that they will become the sort of pariahs that we want them to be. A result is that they may become demonized and considered to be non-human objects. And, of course, once we have reached the stage of viewing them as non-human objects we may now treat them in all manner of ways that are not affected by our conscience.

At an organizational level, it is not unusual for the majority of members of the organization to split off their aggressive and perhaps immoral feelings and to project them into an individual or individuals who act upon these projections. For example, the manager of an organization who wishes to increase sales may develop the notion of misleading potential purchasers. When discussed with colleagues, this may be regarded as an unacceptable practice and feelings of guilt are aroused in even contemplating such action. But the management group does not act in a mature manner by dealing with the reality of the problem. At an unconscious level these unbearable thoughts and feelings are split off, and by the process of projective identification are located in the sales force, which is pressured into taking these feelings in and behaving in a highly unethical manner. Thus, we may have a sales force that carries out the unethical activities for the whole organization and quite happily goes out on the street 'conning' people into signing contracts under the guise of interest documents. This is a collusive process that enables others in the organization to maintain their respectability. At a family level we frequently speak of 'the black sheep of the family'. Here, one family member is used as a repository of all bad feelings, which permits the other members of the family to function without guilt.

In many situations it may be virtually impossible to develop a relationship. All the time we are using other people to enable us to function without guilt, or without anger, or other strong or violent feelings, we cannot begin to develop a relationship with them. We might ask how we are to even begin to understand the views and feelings of the other party in such circumstances. There seems little if any chance of developing the required binocular vision. All the while that we are influenced by processes occurring beneath the surface we will continue to act in this way. However, by means of self-reflection we may be able to access these inner processes and act in a much more mature manner. The 'black sheep of the family' may have been convicted of a crime or have committed some other socially unacceptable behaviour, but this does not necessarily make that person a wholly bad person. There will almost certainly be aspects of that person's personality that are lovable and admirable. To act in a mature manner means taking back our projections from the black sheep and owning them. In doing so we may, of course, have to accept and deal with our own drives and wishes to behave in socially unacceptable ways.

We frequently use others as a means to escape from our own uncomfortable thoughts and feelings. That doesn't mean of course, that we don't still have those thoughts and feelings. What it does do is to leave us in a sort of sanitized, simplistic world where we can 'blame' or 'criticize' others for thoughts and feelings that we are now denying we ever had. By this process we take no authority for such feelings and thoughts and accept no responsibility for those who act on our behalf. For example, when a vicious child killer is arrested members of the public may find that primitive feelings of revenge are mobilized. A result is that we frequently see members of the public shouting, yelling, and banging on the doors of the police van, and these views are frequently reflected in banner headlines in newspapers. It is not unusual that, as part of this process, members of the public may project their feelings into the prison officers or police officers who may then be mobilized to act on these feelings. Yet, when at some stage in the process the child killer appears with a black eye, and prison or police officers are suspected of acting on these primitive feelings of revenge, they are immediately condemned as 'bad apples'. No one in the community accepts responsibility for their part in this process, for their demands for revenge. They now revert to an identity of 'decent citizen'.

In like manner, the members of an organization who have used projective identification to pressure the sales force into adopting unethical behaviour also seek to distance themselves by divesting themselves of these unbearable thoughts and feelings. Doubtless when things go wrong, when the organization is faced with serious complaints and perhaps threats of criminal action, they will deny all knowledge of the practices adopted by the sales force. To say that this would be unfair is to considerably understate the situation. However, much more important is the need for members of organizations to understand that these beneath-the-surface processes can affect anyone unless we are able to reject the projections and leave them with the originators.

Multiple roles and multiple identities

We all take up multiple roles and can be said to have multiple identities. This is something we develop at an early age. Pre-toddler behaviour varies depending on the composition of the group of which he or she is a part. The child acts very differently when in the presence of mother alone, with father, with mother and father, with siblings but without parents, with his or her entire family, and so on. In adult life we behave in a similar manner. When entering a relationship we take on or are allocated a role. There then follows what might be referred to as management of the boundary between person and role. The individual determines what skills, attitudes, feelings, or whatever, he or she will devote to the role and what he or she will withhold.

For example, at work an individual may be a junior manager who takes up the duties of the role in the way delegated to him or her by the line manager. Being a junior manager probably limits his or her capacity to do anything beyond minor decision-making. Outside the work situation the same person may be the Chairman of

his or her Bowls Club, and in this role may take responsibility for and make major decisions concerning the
management of the Club. In each of these roles the individual will need to decide which skills, attitudes, and feelings will be used and which will be withheld.

Hence, we can use these processes to attain some
coherence in the construct or model of what is 'me'. In
reality 'me' is a changing concept whereby what is the
particular me at any particular time is what fits the specific
role. From the current me we get rid of the inconsistent
and conflicting bits that don't fit and attach them to our
constructs of the various 'not mes' with which we popu-
late our environment. Or, to put it another way, we
project these unwanted parts and attach them to others.
Some of these 'not mes', of course, we may have never met
– for example, a president, a film star, or a notorious criminal – but they are nevertheless significant receptacles for
certain projections. To use the language of open systems,
the individual exports chaos from inside and imports
order from outside. So long as this import–export process
is conducted in fantasy it is safe: there can be a satisfactory fit between the picture of self and the picture of
other. But every transaction across the boundary has a
potentiality for disaster: the phantasied boundary between
me and 'not me' may not stand the test of reality. If that
occurs I risk being forced to re-introject the bad bits that
I have projected and to surrender the good bits that I have
introjected.

For example, a university lecturer may approach his
relationship with a new Masters Course as he, the knowing one, who needs to ensure that they, the unknowing
course members, are there to learn from his knowledge.
However, on taking up the role he may discover that

many of the students actually have more knowledge than he does regarding certain aspects of the course. Thus, the phantasied boundary does not stand the test of reality. A further example may concern a member of a finance department who is assigned to an inter-departmental working group and adopts the role that because of his or her superior knowledge and the perceived lack of knowledge of the other members, he or she will become the leader of the working group. When they first meet he or she adopts the role of leader of the group. However, his or her attempts at taking the leadership are totally rejected and others are seen to have different but more relevant knowledge. In effect, he or she is the one with a lack of knowledge and he or she now needs to re-introject the bad bits they have projected and to surrender the good bits that they have introjected.

Identity, therefore, is constantly being negotiated and renegotiated in intersystemic relationships of me and several not mes. We simplify a relationship by drawing a boundary round it, which demarcates this relationship from any other relationship. This relationship (within the boundary) defines the roles that each party will and will not take up in the transaction. Of course, this is not a stable situation but a dynamic and ever-changing process, and no relationship is immune to this process. Each party is engaged in other relationships, involving renegotiation of their personal boundary. These changes require that all relationships require renegotiation because the relationship is also always changing as the other party changes.

Having multiple identities, it follows that each identity can be mobilized according to the experience presented. It may, therefore, also follow that, depending on the identity that is mobilized at any given time, this will affect the way we experience external data, especially other people. Our meaning-making concerning those other people will depend on the identity mobilized at that time. An example may be a father who is being punched by his teenage son, who is beginning to test out his physical and mental strength. The identity mobilized is that of caring father who reasons that violence and punching people is not a good way to behave. This same man is later that day at work in his role of night club bouncer when he is set upon by a group of youths. Here, at this time, the identity mobilized is that of macho man who needs to punch people and physically win to preserve his status. Naturally, the man does not consciously say this is now his identity, it all happens beneath the surface in a spontaneous manner.

The foregoing shows some of the difficulties that may seriously affect and concern us at the interpersonal level of political activity. The politics of identity are indeed a constant element in our lives and such are the possible variables that no matter what our understanding of these phenomena may be, we will be most unlikely to have sufficient awareness to deal with all new and unique situations that arise. But what we can do is to be more aware of the processes and their likely effects.

Identity and unconscious processes

Perhaps a reminder of the unconscious processes involved will help to increase our awareness. The conscious mind develops slowly, and in some respects remains always dominated by the unconscious. According to psychoanalytic theory, as long as we live, our unconscious makes us interpret much of what happens to us in the light of our earlier experiences. For example, our unconscious, on the basis of how we interpreted to ourselves our early experiences with our parents, causes us to believe either that the world is essentially accepting and approving of us or rejecting and disapproving. This extends to our belief that we are good or bad persons; it gives us the feeling that we are or are not competent to deal with life; that we are or are not lovable; even whether we will be rewarded or disappointed.

Such far-reaching attitudes are formed on the basis of extremely vague feelings that we nevertheless experienced most strongly at a time when, because our reasoning abilities were as yet undeveloped, we could not yet comprehend the meaning of what was happening to us. And since these attitudes that continue to dominate our experiences originate in our unconscious, we do not know what caused them and why they are so convincing to us. Yet, convincing and influential they are for each individual. So, for example, we may go into a relationship with a clear belief that the other party does not like us. There is no basis for this belief in the behaviour of the other party to the relationship. It is entirely the work of processes beneath the surface.

Identity and values

Each of us also develops our own set of values. By means of the primitive process of introjection we take in values which then form internal mental images that become part of our stock of knowledge. This process starts in infancy and continues through school and other education and is added to in our working lives. It is perhaps important at this juncture to bear in mind that we are all unique. It is true that we may share values with others with whom we attended school or college, and may share values with those in our respective work disciplines. Thus, in a large organization HR professionals may share some values concerning their discipline. For example, they may all have values regarding equality and encouraging diversity. However, other parts of the organization may have no such values. Sales, for example, may simply be concerned with values that are about achieving financial success at almost any cost. It is not difficult to realize that in such circumstances the interface between these employees may be a source of conflict.

Identity and emotions

More importantly, our unique internal mental images, which are, of course, unconscious, may include feelings that will influence our behaviour. Thus, at a deep emotional level we may find certain behaviour of others abhorrent. As above, we may not know why such behaviours are so convincing to us as we are likely to be unaware of their origins. For all of us the development of what is commonly called the conscience results in the ideal conscience, a sense of ideals and positive morality – a pattern of what to do; and the persecutory conscience, a sense of guilt and negative morality – of what not to do. Conscience may evoke particularly strong feelings that are unique to each individual. In workplace meetings we frequently hear expressions from individuals such as, 'I don't feel comfortable with that'. On many of those occasions the reason for the discomfort is because what is being discussed is contrary to the individual's conscience.

Seldom is the real reason made explicit and frequently the discomfort is overridden by others who do not share the same values and whose conscience is clear.

The politics of identity may present a huge potential for disaster if we are not sufficiently aware of the likely possibilities. I wonder how many times people have met to discuss important issues and left feeling that they had developed a good working relationship and a satisfactory outcome only to find that subsequent feedback suggests the contrary. If we are to solely rely on what people – including ourselves – say, we shall never, for example, be exploring respective values. In many professions values are an important and valuable part of their discipline. For example, the medical profession is strongly influenced by the Hippocratic Oath; lawyers by a code of representing the client's case even if the client is a dislikeable person; and members of religious organizations by an adherence to a belief and following of their respective faith. In these instances, respective values may be clear and understand-able to even those who are not part of the profession. That is not to say that there may not still be problems in devel-oping relationships.

Political differences will not only exist beneath the surface, they may also develop at a purely cognitive level. The nature of overt political relationships and relatedness may cause us to have difficulty in communicating and relating at either a cognitive or experiential level. Difficulties that are occurring above the surface can usually be discussed using a shared language. Never-theless, many cognitive differences may also trigger strong differences at the emotional level. They may trigger our values, our conscience, and all manner of emotional experiences that are present beneath the surface. But no matter what the nature of the political relationships and relatedness, at a cognitive level they will bear no comparison to the problems experienced by those originating from beneath the surface.

Faced with these complicated and difficult situations, the reader could be forgiven if he or she was feeling terribly despondent. It would not be surprising if you were not asking where we might start to make things possible. The simple answer is that we can only start with ourselves. Let none of us be under any illusion that this is anything but hard work. All of us have to constantly struggle to understand ourselves better, not the least because our efforts to achieve greater clarity about ourselves make it possible for us to achieve clarity in our relation to other important people, with a consequent enrichment of our life. Such understanding of ourselves around some issue of a relationship cannot be handed to us by someone else, no matter how great their expertise may be; it can be achieved only by ourselves, as we struggle to remove whatever has obscured this understanding from our consciousness. Only our own efforts to achieve such higher comprehension will lead to permanent personal growth. All that someone else or, for that matter, any book can do – including this one – is to address some of the overall problems: their origin, significance, meaning, and particularly, possible ways of thinking about them.

There is a further specific aspect concerning the interpersonal level of political activity that will be explored in the next sub-section: that concerning power and authority. As with politics, power and authority do not exist in the private world of 'self'; they are relational concepts that require us to have an interaction with another person or another group. The potency of authority lies in the images of authority that are formed in childhood and which persist in adult life.

5. Power and authority

Whether we like it or not it is impossible to escape the notion of power and authority. Any cursory reflection on our history will show us that natural social groups have developed in the form of families, clans, tribes, states, and nations. Within these groups, superior–subordinate relationships have developed in the form of status and role systems. Based on any number of characteristics, power structures evolve naturally, and they in turn are perpetuated by tradition. Indeed, it may be hard to imagine that the human community could proceed in its endeavours without an institutionalized power structure, which we call authority. However, as in so many similar conceptual frameworks, what is required is a workable compromise.

On the one hand, we need enough authority to ensure co-operative action and progress towards group goals. But on the other hand, we also want to encourage individuality, creativity, and innovation. At one extreme, anarchy is inconceivable; but so is the other extreme, authoritarianism. It might be helpful in considering these extremes if we bear in mind the distinctions between power and authority. These are frequently used as interchangeable concepts, but I would suggest that this can only lead to confusion and emotional strife.

Taking a fairly traditional view of power we can say that it is essentially a capacity that one person has to influence the behaviour of another person or persons so that

111

the other person or persons do something that they would not otherwise have done. This would seem to imply that power is a potential that needs to be exercised to be effective and that it relies upon a dependence relationship. Various sources and bases of power have been identified, some of which are as follows: reward power; knowledge power; coercive power; position power; personal power; expert power; and opportunity power. In short, we might consider all of these under the heading of 'resource power'; at different times and at different places the resource will vary from, say, reward to expertise, or whatever, but it all seems to come back to the resources of the powerful.

'Authority' may be seen as a neutral term, but such is the emotion surrounding the exercise of authority that there are many misconceptions. A common error is for authority to be confused with both influence and authoritarianism. In effect, 'authority' means that the person or persons with authority have the sole right to do anything within the terms of their authority. This is in contrast to influence, which may be effected over any area but the influencer may have to make reference to someone or something else for the necessary approvals. In other words, influence and, it follows, power, may not be coexistent with authority. Moving now to authoritarianism, this is simply a particular kind of authority that exists at the expense of freedom. On the one hand, authoritarianism results from an obsession with hierarchical relationships to the degree that superiors eschew consultation with subordinates. But on the other hand, subordinates are disposed towards zealous obedience to hierarchic superiors. Thus, we may end up with a collusive dynamic leading to authoritarianism.

112

Managerial authority

As with power, to gain a deeper understanding of authority, it will help to explore something of its sources and foundations. In practice, authority – the right to carry out task leadership – stems from various sources. The most obvious, and most often referred to, is the notion of authority as institutionalized power, which is established legally to achieve the objectives of a formal organization. It is based on legal foundations, for example, legislation, articles of incorporation, partnership agreements, and bye-laws that define an organization's mission and empower its members to carry out its activities. The fountainhead of all authority in a private enterprise such as a partnership is the owner(s), and in a corporation, it is the shareholders. It is they who delegate the authority to managers and leaders and, most importantly, set the boundaries of that authority. What we are referring to here is 'managerial authority', which refers to that part of the leader's authority that has been delegated to them by the institution they work in.

In many organizations the extent and details of this sort of authority is contained in a Job Description and perhaps a Job Specification. These documents, taken together, formally set out the boundaries of the authority that is being delegated to the individual manager. Whatever the 'job description' may be, it is important to understand that it concerns authority for matters that have been delegated by someone who, in turn, has the right to delegate that degree of authority. We may conclude, therefore, that authority is the application of power by the manager as a means of political action that is aimed at following and achieving goals linked to the organization's primary task. Authority may thus be considered functional and rationally related to organizational functioning. Power used by a manager in support of achieving organizational goals and tasks is legitimate and in the interests of the organization.

As we have already stated, power as influence may be affected over any area, but if it is to be legitimately used the influencer may have to make reference to someone or something else for the necessary approvals. In other words, influence may not be coexistent with authority. Where power is used outside the legitimate boundaries of authority it may be considered an abuse of power. Using power in a political sense of organizational functioning, we can say that where behaviour is carried out by individuals or groups in the pursuit of individual interests or goals, such as an attempt to influence other members to do something contrary to the aims of the organization, this will be an abuse of authority. In that regard institutional politics may be considered a form of rivalry, a challenge to the legitimate authority of the organization, to determine which members of the organization are most powerful – a classic power struggle. In like manner, where an individual uses power in an authoritarian manner that impinges on the freedom of others, this is equally illegitimate use, and an abuse, of power.

Leadership authority

Managerial authority is but one source of power. 'Leadership authority' is very different, and refers to that aspect of the manager or leader's authority that is derived from the recognition of other organizational members that they have the capacity to carry out the task. Here, I am defining 'leadership' as 'always involving attempts on the part of the leader (influencer) to affect (influence) the behaviour of a follower'. However, I have to confess to a degree of discomfort with the term 'follower'. My discomfort is with the connotation of a set and determined hierarchical relationship between the leader and their followers. I have in mind a picture of the manager being the leader, the one with all the knowledge, the one with all the ideas, and the followers being expected to thank the leader profusely and blindly follow whatever they say. This is getting very close to the notion of the authoritarian leader who ignores the freedom of others. I much prefer to think of leaders and 'joiners', of any member of the team leading on a particular issue and others (including the manager) joining them to further consider and build on the idea that the team member seeks to influence them about.

Leadership authority differs from management authority in a highly significant way. Management authority is clearly delegated to the manager only. He or she can delegate responsibility for this authority but the manager and only the manager is still accountable for performance. With regard to leadership authority, this can rest with the manager but it does not have to. Any member of the organization can take their authority for leadership. Indeed, in any organization that values their personnel all will be encouraged to take on leadership authority.

Managerial and leadership authority reinforce each other; both are, in turn, dependent upon other sources of authority, such as the leader's technical knowledge, their personality, their human skills, and the social tasks and responsibilities they assume outside the organization. The manager or leader is responsible not only to the -

115

organization but also to the other staff, to their professional and ethical values, to the community, and to society at large; responsibility and accountability represent the reciprocal obligation of the manager to the sources of their authority. The management structure can be considered functional when the distribution and delegation of authority, task performance, and task monitoring are matched by appropriate – that is, sufficient and stable but not excessive – investment of authority in managerial leaders at all levels.

The true nature of authority is that the leader or manager is able to directly affect the behaviour of a member of an organization if they possess authority with respect to that member. But the real source of authority possessed by a manager or leader lies in the acceptance of its exercise by those who are subject to it. A manager may have the authority to tell workers or staff how to carry out their task or what to do, but it is the workers or staff who determine the authority that the manager or leader may wield. In effect, formal authority is nominal authority. It only becomes real when it is accepted. No matter that the manager may tell them to do something, or demand that they do, it may all be in vain. A manager or leader may possess formal authority, but this is meaningless unless that authority can be effectively used. And it can be so used only if it is accepted by the other team members. Thus, to be effective, formal authority must coincide with authority determined by its acceptance. The latter defines the useful limits of the former. We may usefully summarize the situation with the slogan: 'leadership is nothing without followership (or joiners)'.

Faced with a bullying manager, staff may find it such an unbearable experience that they identify with the aggressor and become like the bullying manager. In this case the whole group or department of the organization may ride roughshod over those inside or outside the organization that they have relationships with. Apart from the obvious result of poor relationships and bad reputation, there is another more important outcome. Identification with the aggressor means giving up certain aspects of self and repressing them into our unconscious. But, of course, they still remain in our pool of internalized knowledge and feelings. The mental conflict caused by adopting behaviour that is not really acceptable will put a considerable strain on those concerned and sickness may be a result. The unbearable thoughts and feelings arising from being bullied may also be dealt with by other defence mechanisms. However, where workers or staff are able to stay in touch with reality, where they refuse to be bullied, where they take their own authority to not respond to a manager who is abusing his power by acting outside his or her authority, the bully may be left with no authority.

In most instances the manager or leader may, on the face of things, have immense authority. They may have the right to hire and fire; or to reward and punish workers or staff without referral to anyone else. But, in practice, although they may demand or insist, there is no guarantee that other workers or staff will fully comply. The concept 'authority', then, describes an interpersonal relationship in which one individual, the organizational member, accepts a decision made by another individual, the manager or leader, permitting that decision directly to affect their behaviour. A team member always has an opportunity, with respect to a decision made by the manager or leader directly to affect his behaviour, to accept or reject that decision. It is appreciated, of course, that such rejection by

117

the team member may result in dismissal, or, at the very least, the need for a voluntary leaving.

Dependency and other beneath-the-surface influences

Thus far, this has been a fairly traditional exploration of power and authority. But we have already been alerted to some of the difficulties that may arise from behaviour beneath the surface. To appreciate just how important the notion of authority is we only have to reflect on the fact that we all start our lives dependent on authority figures. We can, therefore, begin to have an appreciation of the likely effect that authority will have on all of us throughout our lives. Starting our lives dependent on authority figures can have a lasting influence on our relationships and relatedness to other authority figures that we come across in later life. If the authority figure, the father or the mother, is experienced, introjected, and becomes an internal object that is feared or disliked for some reason, our meaning-making process regarding future experiences of authority figures may be to perceive them also as feared or disliked.

For example, seen in the light of the problems of identity, the 'me' who is perhaps a social worker may bring to the relationship with his or her senior social worker the belief that he or she is oppressed, insecure, and looking to the manager to make most major decisions. In addition, they may seek to project into the manager feelings of competence and power so that he or she acts in an overpowering manner. The beneath-the-surface processes being unconsciously designed to ensure that previously expected conditions are replicated in the current situation.

Where we have experienced a parent as controlling and perhaps aggressive, we may develop a mental image of an authority figure possessing all these qualities and this mental image will be associated with all the feelings that helped to create that image. As a young child we may have been terrified that we were for ever going to be berated and slapped down on every occasion that we attempted to assert our freedom. And on the occasions that this occurred we may have suffered extreme feelings of frustration, anger, and even murderous thoughts regarding the object that was doing the controlling. When later in life we are confronted with a teacher, acquaintance, or employer who triggers these feelings we may treat that person as if they were the parent.

I feel sure that all who are managers have experienced the member of staff who, no matter what the circumstances, always seems to be difficult and unco-operative. Seen in a non-reflective way the manager may simply consider this as a personal matter and that the member of staff simply does not like him or her. However, if we are able to gain an understanding of beneath-the-surface processes we may consider that relationships with the member of staff may be evoking feelings developed with a significant other from a previous relationship. And this is why the employee responds in such a difficult manner. If we are non-reflective we can simply view him or her as a difficult person; but if we are reflective, as a person who is sometimes difficult. This latter approach may eventually result in changed behaviour by the employee.

Beneath the adult struggles with power, right, and legitimacy, there remain these archaic images of what strength and power should be, so that as adults we are interpreting not what is really occurring now but what

119

once was in our lives. It is rather like reading a hidden text with more powerful messages. What happened to us in childhood is that every action of our parents contributed to our image of their strength. The infant has no standards for judgement, no way of separating his or her self from the parent; whatever the parent does is potent, and the infant cannot imagine, in its egoistic universe, that the parent does anything that has no effect on itself. Is Mummy depressed? It must be my fault. Is Daddy angry? It must be because of something I have done. When they punish me, I don't understand the reasons, but I must have been bad. Do they love me? Then they must love me absolutely.

At a later stage the child simply competes with the parent of the same sex, a competition with a naturally ambivalent outcome. The little boy wants to take the place of his father, but does not want to lose his father's love. At still later stages adolescents divorce themselves from obedience to their parents, but none.the.less want the parents to care for them whenever they are in need. An adult would come to admit the strength as well as the limits of his parents, but would see the strength on its own terms, as a force which belonged to them, made him, but is now not part of his own. This is all part and parcel of developing personality boundaries. This does not mean that as adults we shall always be able to make decisions that are totally free of other people. For example, in the work situation an individual may find the manager's approach totally abhorrent and would have a strong need to challenge him or her. However, a stronger need may be to remain working with the organization. In these circumstances, he or she may blot out the feelings associated with the manager by means of denial.

Competition

The exercise of power and authority will frequently evoke feelings of competition. Groups and organizations may evoke feelings of sibling rivalry or simply those concerning our desires to gain favourable responses from our mother. Authority and decision-making in groups and organizations requires that formal authority needs to be taken by the manager or other leader and that others need in turn to give their authority to the manager or other leader. Where this is not possible because of the competitive dynamics existing in the group or organization, there is likely to be stagnation, no progress, and no decisions, or perhaps more accurately, no real decisions. Competition can prevent the giving or taking of authority; for example, an individual may withhold their authority because, at a conscious or unconscious level, they want to be the leader.

Where competition is not confronted and remains unresolved it may result in self-exclusion and/or exclusion of others. For example, where members of several disciplines are working in a joint team, should the head of one discipline be highly competitive and seek to be the leader in opposition to the appointed leader, the team will be unable to operate as a team. The head of discipline who fails to authorize the appointed leader will self-exclude him or herself and probably the other members of the discipline. I have often heard managers talking enthusiastically about 'healthy competition being good for an organization'. Taking a reflective stance, I am much more concerned that beneath-the-surface processes concerning competition may be extremely unhealthy for the organization and its members.

121

We are never totally independent, even after 'me' and 'not me' have been established. As in the maternal and family holding environment, we are ambivalent about authority. At one level we are always in danger of regressing to the comfortable dependent position. Doubtless, many of us can reflect on situations when we did not support the relevant authority figure, yet we decided to go along with them for an easy life. At another level we are at once ravenous for the comfort of a stronger person and in a rage against the very strength they so desire. Given the infant's journey from dependency to individuation this may not be surprising. The ambivalent nature of this struggle between a sense of freedom and the fear of abandonment is likely to be repeated and experienced in later experiences. Thus, we may welcome the strong leader for providing a framework for our support but we may reject this same strong leader because they are interfering with our sense of freedom.

In effect, what people are willing to believe is not simply a matter of the credibility or legitimacy of the ideas, rules, and persons offered to them. It is also a matter of them needing to believe. What they want from an authority is as important as what the authority has to offer. Where there is a great deal of anxiety and dependence they may seek out a leader who offers them the security of a way out of their discomfort. In this sort of situation those concerned may be vulnerable to a leader intent on abusing the power afforded him by the dependent others: we may be attracted to strong figures even if they are not legitimate. This is a collusive process whereby a manager or assumed leader who is obsessed with maintaining total control is supported in this use of power by others who are disposed toward zealous obedience to hierarchic superiors. It is in this way that we may end up with a collusive dynamic leading to authoritarianism. Anyone who has a knowledge of the situation in Germany in the 1930s will be aware that this is precisely how Hitler and the Nazi Party came to power with such horrific results. Doubtless we may be able to recall other relevant examples in organizations and institutions.

The authority situation between workers or staff and manager is always likely to recreate, to some extent, in those involved a dependency situation analogous to one's infancy and will thus tend to reactivate the characteristic way of handling problems that was developed at that time. As the child sought help from the parents, a team member seeks help and assistance from the manager. Even a simple request for something like a favourable agreement on financial terms places the team member in a subordinate position to a person in authority. When the help requested is more extensive than this, the feeling of dependency is proportionately greater. It is impossible for workers or staff to place themselves for long in such a dependency situation without there being some level of transference to this new situation of their infantile attitudes. Part of this transference will be positive, corresponding to the love felt for the parental figure; part of it will be negative, corresponding to the fear of anyone possessing such power over one's own destinies.

In all authority relationships there are likely to be difficulties. Almost every situation that involves hierarchical relationships will result in each individual's unique personality being of paramount importance in the way they will respond to those seeking to exercise power and authority. This is so whether we are referring to a parent–teacher meeting; a tenants' group meeting; a

123

formal work situation; a family; or wherever. Each unique individual will bring their own meaning-making self to the situation and this will affect the relationships. By way of example, a manager or friend may seek to offer a helping hand to someone by offering advice and support in achieving a task. Unknown to the helper, when the person was young he had experienced his father deserting him and the rest of the family, a result being that this caused the child to see all male authority figures as 'bad' and 'not to be trusted'. Faced with someone who triggers their unconscious image of father, they treat the 'helper' as if they are father. They put into practice their tried and tested plans for dealing with untrustworthy authority figures, which might involve espousing agreement but choosing to ignore the advice.

Exercising authority

I have thus far mainly concentrated on those who are subjected to authority: those who are being managed or influenced. I now want to refer to those who are taking authority. Taking personal or collective authority can be a very anxiety-provoking situation. Making a wrong decision may result in some very serious resource implications in human and or financial terms. In all manner of organizations, environmental circumstances will always influence the behaviour of those in authority and the mutual influence arising out of the relatedness of other groups may be both positive and negative. A good example might concern a manager in the steel industry in the late 1990s; such a manager would have been aware that raw steel prices could fluctuate on a daily basis and would be influenced by political as well as economic influences. In these circumstances there was a constant fear of making a decision that resulted in a financial loss; and a subsequent constant anxiety as to survival. Faced with such anxiety, this would have brought into play many of the defences referred to in Section One.

Past influences on those taking authority will also be important. For example, I have referred briefly to those who may abuse power, especially those who seek to control others in an authoritarian manner. This, of course, is not the only category of person who is in the position of exercising power and authority. There will be a wide range of helpful and positive individuals who will all be influenced by their unique personality. This may include those who are guided by an internal world that seeks to encourage co-operation and the avoidance of conflict in a way that corresponds to the love felt for the parental figure.

People fear exercising power when they do not have a sufficiently good internal image of their character, and when they feel they are fundamentally bad. If they feel they are partly bad and mean, they are reluctant to wield power, fearing that they will be unable to contain their anger and will therefore hurt others and be hurt in turn. Aggression and power conjure up an imagined world where people persecute one another. In psychological terms we can say that such persons have too punishing or too harsh a superego, a conscience that is too strict and constantly reprimands them for the smallest misdeeds or simply for bad or forbidden thoughts. An example may be a situation where a team is constantly failing to achieve at the level required. The manager is angry, frustrated, and concerned that things have to change. However, instead of expressing his or her feelings in an assertive manner, he or she simply sympathizes with their predicament. He or she is scared that they will become violent and aggressive and will therefore not take their authority.

As has been stated, everyone gradually develops, through years of experience, characteristic ways of relating to people. These will all affect the way we take up our authority and this will be further influenced by the unique environment in which we find ourselves at any given time. I have already referred to relationships that are based on unconscious displacements from early life and those that are primarily reactions to the real attitudes and behaviour of the present day person. In the next sub-section I continue by distinguishing between reality and phantasy relationships.

6. Reality and phantasy relationships

Reality relationships

A reality relationship is based on our conscious appreciation of the other party to a relationship as they really are. It differs from what has come to be known as 'transference' – the unconscious projection on to the other party of our attitudes toward a potent figure of our early childhood. In these circumstances, we are not in a 'reality' relationship with the other party but we are, in fact, albeit unconsciously, relating to them as if they were a totally different person; we literally project on to the other party the personality of some other person from the past and treat the other party as that other person.

To put it in the context of our previous discussions, when the other person and their behaviour are compared with our internal pool of knowledge and feelings they trigger thoughts and feelings of a potent figure of our past. For example, if we perceive that they are behaving in an uncaring manner, not only do we identify him or her with some potent person from the past but we then actually treat that other person as if they are the person from the past. In doing so we evoke all the feelings that were experienced in the original situation. If at that time we were angry, jealous, envious, hostile, or whatever, we shall now have the same feelings about this person.

In cases where we are relatively mature, if our contacts with the other party have mainly been seen as mutually beneficial, we will tend to develop a satisfactory rapport; whereas if our contacts have mainly been experienced as irritating to one or both parties, they may lead to an acrimonious relationship. In either case they are apt to be fairly direct results of reality factors in the immediate situation. In the case of such reality-adjusted behaviour, we can respond by giving attention to the reality situation. In other words, our perception will unconsciously lead us to deal with the person as he or she is. If the reality factors that have already affected us have been favourable, we can take advantage of the initial rapport thus created to get on with the work. If we encounter antagonism, we will need first to look at the factual nature of the immediately preceding experiences. In such cases we will need to seek in ourselves and in the surrounding environment the objective situations, delays, misunderstandings, and so on, that are occasioning this negative reaction, and will seek to remove them and replace them with stimuli conducive to satisfaction, liking, and trust.

If we can control and manage our feelings we will most likely be able to deal with the relationship and any

127

ensuing problems as reality factors. This means that we shall be able to live with our seemingly unbearable thoughts and feelings and not adopt beneath-the-surface processes as a means of avoiding reality. If we take the example of a non-reflective social worker who is trying to develop a relationship with a client, he or she may regard an acrimonious situation as a sign that the client is unco-operative. A different reflective social worker, presented with the same circumstances, may take the acrimonious situation as a sign that there are real differences to be explored and clarified before the relationship can develop helpfully.

Phantasy relationships

In most people, reality factors, that is, the real situation and the real attitude of both parties, are the determining ones in establishing the quality of a relationship. Our feelings towards the other party are fairly directly caused, are conscious, and are subject to relatively easy control. Genuine *transference* feelings, on the other hand, although they may be currently stimulated, are remotely caused, are largely unconscious, and present a huge potential for misunderstanding. When our problem is in part a person-ality one, or requires considerable time for its solution, the influences that bring about transference are increased, and transference occurs to a correspondingly greater degree. This is behaviour emanating from beneath the surface.

Several examples have previously been provided but it may be helpful to take a new example, that of a police officer who is using his authority to instruct a motorist to move an illegally parked vehicle. As sometimes occurs, the presence of the obvious and formal authority figure that is a police officer may evoke in the motorist beneath-the-surface processes connected with a potent authority figure from the past. In doing so, all the feelings connected with this past experience will also be evoked and this may include feelings of hate and hostility, which will be directed at the police officer. It seems needless to say that this may present a huge potential for misunderstanding.

Often transference feelings are not direct projections of a parent or other childhood figure on to the other party. In the course of our life we may have 'projected' this momentous early figure on to a number of other people – teachers, acquaintances, employers, and so on. Subsequently, the projection on to the other party may then be from one of these later persons, or derivatives, as they are called. In the successive transfers that have occurred, the original figure may have become modified or even quite distorted. Thus, the other party may be the recipient of the feelings we have currently towards an aunt, a teacher, or a child, as well as, or instead of, those we had in childhood towards a parent.

Fortunately, changes can and do occur in our attitudes, behaviour, and personalities throughout life. But as we become older, far-reaching changes become much more difficult to achieve, as each year we become more settled into seeing and doing things in customary ways. In short, we become less flexible. Changes that may occur when we are older are likely to affect only limited areas of our personalities and our lives. The importance of early experiences thus rests on the fact that they set the stage for all that comes later, and the earlier the experiences are, the more emphatic their influence.

In the same way that we reflect on our experiences of past relationships we can also helpfully reflect on the way

129

these matters were dealt with by those who were senior, older, or more influential than us: our parents, teachers, managers, and leaders. Knowing which of their methods we liked or disliked can be helpful in guiding our actions now that we are taking our own authority in relationships. But, whether or not we approved of what our parents, teachers, managers, or leaders did in any particular situation, their methods will have made a deep and lasting impression, and will continue to carry the aura of authority, irrespective of whether we have incorporated their ways of acting into our own behaviour or continued to resent them. Thus, in the same way that our parents influenced our development, so also will other authority figures influence us later in life.

Mention has already been made of the situation where an abused child becomes an abusing parent. When we internalize the methods and behaviour of those who were influential in some way, this object who was an abusing authority figure remains in our pool of internalized knowledge and is liable to be evoked when similar situations are perceived later in life. When we become teachers, parents, managers, or leaders and are faced with difficult and anxiety-provoking situations that may evoke past experiences, we, too, may become a bullying authority figure. Clearly, this is not a reality relationship, and for the person being bullied it may be highly confusing.

It will be appreciated that in developing any relationship this may pose considerable difficulty, and will require a high degree of self-awareness and reflection if we are to understand our own dominant behaviours. However, it also presents potential problems in our dealings with others. Hopefully, most relationships will be with well-adjusted individuals who have their own high level of self-awareness and will be operating on a reality basis; but there will undoubtedly be some relationships where the behaviour of the other party will be unconsciously triggered by past experience and the other party will unconsciously treat the relationship on a non-reality basis.

When faced with a difficult relationship that is simply not making sense, we might need to consider who the other party is identifying us with. But, unless we know the other person exceedingly well, we are most unlikely to know who we are being identified with. We will not have access to the unconscious processes and feelings of the other person, but we may treat the sense data as a clue that this is not a reality based experience. That is, of course, if we do not take in the projections of the other person and become mobilized into a role such as that of an angry and difficult person who needs to be slapped down.

The real danger in these situations is when we equate current behaviour as being synonymous with the individual. When we take a non-reflective stance we are likely to take things at face value, to see and hear what is in front of us. In this way we are then in danger of comparing that data with our pool of internalized knowledge and feelings and classifying someone on the basis of that relatively scanty data. By taking a reflective stance we can stay with the reality of the situation and, working from the presented data that tells us that the other person is angry or hostile, try to gain an understanding of why this is the case. When we initiate a joint exploration with the other individual we may discover that the reasons for the anger and hostility have a reality base. Where this is not so clear it may cause us to consider that the anger and hostility have their origin in phantasy. Knowing this can help us to try to continue the relationship at a reality level.

All of us have phantasies about the ideas and feelings with which we invest any new situation, about ourselves, about others, about the nature of the relationship, and the relationship between others. By phantasies I mean mental concepts not based on reality. This requires that we not only need to understand relationships with others but also our relatedness to those other people. That is, the way that emotions and phantasies affect the way they relate to other team members. Where, for example, things are not going well, a manager may become increasingly anxious and develop a phantasy that the staff are not pulling their weight. In reality the staff may have been putting all possible effort into their task. But the phantasy will predominate the thinking and the manager may treat the staff as if they were shirkers.

This can work both ways, and it may be the case that the staff may develop negative phantasies about the manager or leader. For example, they may develop the phantasy that the manager or leader 'does not care about others' or that the manager or leader 'is angry with us because we disagreed with him or her in the last meeting'. The reality may be somewhat different, but in such cases, the likely outcome is that the staff will not have any desire to communicate with the manager or leader for fear of the results. In all these circumstances there is a very real potential for conflict and disaster. Even situations where we have developed apparently well-founded relationships with others can suddenly develop in a seemingly inexplicable manner and then we are left confused and shocked.

We live in a world where all manner of political activity, especially that at the level of interpersonal political activity, may complicate and confuse the reality. Without a relatively stable shared frame of reference based on reality we will experience problems of communication and the expectations of either or both parties working together may not be met. This may, in turn, lead to a breakdown in the relationship, which is even more likely to occur in a situation where trust does not exist. Trust is an elusive phenomenon and it is difficult to describe precisely what we mean by the term. In the next sub-section I attempt to gain a deeper understanding of this important dynamic.

7. Trust

Trust is another phenomenon that is an ever-present dynamic in relationships. In almost any situation trust will be a key factor, but what do we understand it to be? We all know what the experience of trust is like and we can all recount situations where we were able to feel both trusting and trusted. When we explore those situations we can begin to appreciate that for trust to exist there needs to be a relationship between a human being and another object – usually another human being. Even if we speak of trusting ourselves, it is in relation to something or someone else. We might, therefore, as our first point of understanding, posit that trust is a relational concept.

When we continue to reflect on our experiences we will also realize that trust is not a continuous experience. A frequent comment about trust is that it is difficult to achieve and easy to lose. We will also be aware that trust does not automatically remain once it exists; it is something that may weaken in experience along a range from complete trust to distrust. We might take, then, as our second point of understanding, that trust is a dynamic process. And, as a third point, that trust is situationally specific or unique. In other words, no two situations are the same when it comes to trust.

Continuing our reflection of previous experiences we might ask, how do we describe trust? And here I am left in difficulty because words do not seem adequate to describe this phenomenon. However, this may in itself be valuable as it points us in the direction of feelings and emotions. Like other emotions, for example, love, we know what it is when we experience it but words are inadequate to cover the range, quality, and multitude of related emotions. We might take as a further point, then, that trust is a mainly emotional state.

Further reflection will clearly inform us that trust does not just happen. It needs to be based on positive experiences that encourage within us this emotional state of trust. These may be experiences over a period of time or, perhaps, experiences of such a quality that we feel secure enough to trust another object, usually another person. We might, then, also say that trust develops as a result of our positive experience of other people.

Trust does not have to be mutual. We can trust someone or something else without the need for them trusting us. However, for a genuine relationship we might say that there is a need to trust and to be trusted.

Characteristics of trust

To summarize, we might say that trust is characterized by the following:

- it is a relational concept;
- it is a dynamic process;

- it is situationally specific or unique;
- it is a mainly emotional state;
- it develops as a result of our experience of other people.

This has been a useful introductory exploration of the phenomenon that we call 'trust', but it will be helpful for our later application if we can obtain a deeper understanding. In the process of doing so, I shall seek to answer the question, 'how does trust develop?' To help find answers to this question you will not be surprised that I shall start with an exploration of the role of trust in our very first relationship – that between mother and infant.

Trust in the maternal holding environment

The issue of trust goes right to the heart of our very first experience as humans, the relationship between mother and child, and it is felt that this relationship will provide us with the deeper understanding that we seek. As has been stated regarding the notion of relatedness, there is never 'just an infant'. Intrinsic to the picture of infancy is a caretaker who, from the point of view of the infant, is something more than an 'other person' who relates to and assists the growth of that infant. The early relation in what I shall refer to as the maternal holding environment is characterized by infantile dependency. A relationship grows through the ability of both parties to experience and adjust to each other's natures. The relationship develops through the infant getting to know the mother as she presents herself to interpret and meet his or her needs, which are emotional as well as physical. The baby needs to have not only food and comfort but also the security of a loving relationship in which he or she can grow and learn to know him or her self and a range of feelings.

Developmental psychology has demonstrated that the infant has an innate capacity to seek out and make use of the various characteristics of a human caretaker. The infant prefers the human face and voice above other visual and auditory stimuli and feels comforted by rhythmic rocking, the sound of mother's heart, and the familiar smell of her body. Yet, the nature of this fit between what the infant is reaching out for and what the mother can provide is not a static phenomenon; it is intrinsically dynamic, providing the basis for a subtle reciprocal interaction between mother and baby that contains within it the potential for increasingly complex exchanges.

'Basic trust'

For the infant to develop there is a need for a 'basic trust' and for what has been termed 'a good enough mother'. This basic trust is developed as a result of the infant's perceived experience of the maternal holding environment. Within the trusted framework of their relationship, and by the kind of administration that in its quality combines sensitive care of the baby's individual needs and a firm sense of personal trustworthiness, the mother creates a sense of trust in her child. This forms the basis in the child for a sense of identity that will later combine a sense of 'being all right' of being oneself, and of becoming what other people trust one will become.

Here we are referring to experience in the first year of the infant's life. Being part of the earliest experience this will be highly influential and will set the stage for all that is to come. Trust, being a vital part of this early experience, will therefore play an important part in all our lives. With it being a mainly emotional phenomena we may also discover that trust is likely to be exceptionally influential and may be associated with many other unconscious internal objects. This may account for the sort of responses that we hear about relationships where one party may say something like 'I don't know why but I don't like him', or 'I can't put my finger on it but there's something about him that I don't like'.

Maternal empathy

Another concept we need to consider in regard to this relationship is that of maternal empathy, by which we mean that the mother intuitively knows what to do, she is able to empathize, to 'feel into' the child, to truly experience what the infant is experiencing. Empathy has been described as 'feeling into', that is, the ability to perceive the subjective experience of another person. It is posited that empathy is a process where we imitate the distress or elation of another, which then evokes the same feelings in us. In family life we frequently empathize with the pain and suffering or sheer delight of our parents, siblings, or children. A 'good enough' mother will be experienced by the infant as 'trustworthy'. Put another way, trust develops as a result of our experience of other people.

From this very first relationship – that between mother and infant – it seems clear that 'trust' is a vital and important element in the development of the infant. Starting from a dependent position, the mother provides an environment that we might refer to as a 'trusted framework' that enables the infant to be able to trust and be trusted. To achieve this trusted framework the mother must provide physical and psychological support and, most importantly, provide for the infant's emotional needs. To achieve this she must provide maternal empathy or, put another way, she must communicate with the infant at an emotional level. There will then develop what has been referred to as 'basic trust', a requirement for the healthy development of the infant.

The foregoing has provided us with a deeper understanding of some of the requirements of a trusting relationship. I would suggest that the requirement for meeting the infant's emotional needs is a key factor in understanding the development of trust in all relationships. Doubtless, emotions have been a factor in relationships since time began; however, it is only in recent times that the issue of 'emotions' has become a significant part of social and management thinking. There is now a better understanding of the subject matter but this may not have translated into actions. In the following paragraphs it is intended to show how some of the problems of trust in relationships can be overcome by developing what has been referred to as a facilitating environment.

Development of trust – a facilitating environment

If we are to provide a facilitating environment and to develop a healthy, trusting, relationship, we need to be attuned to the other party both psychologically and socially. Trust in interpersonal relationships is essential if full and open communication is to occur in a relationship. An open, non-manipulative sharing of information is required for the effective solving of task problems. This all sounds simple, but as is the position in the maternal holding environment, trust does not exist automatically; it has to be developed from experience. In the relationship situation, much will depend on the sort of facilitating environment that is developed by the individuals concerned. Relationship orientations that are based on the manipulation of others generate widespread distrust at all levels. This distrust of one party by the other may be one of the initial problems encountered in any relationship. Trust is exceedingly difficult to come by and very easy to lose.

If these needs are to be met, the conditions required are very much the same as those required in the maternal holding environment. The parties to a relationship can respond in responsible and productive ways to an environment in which they are given an opportunity to grow and mature. A self-actualizing man or woman is an individual behaving at his or her most productive level. An individual is most likely to behave in self-actualizing ways if the culture in which they are operating is characterized by openness, trust, a willingness to confront conflictual issues, and if they have challenging goals. In other words, in a relationship we are looking to develop a sort of 'neutral' culture, a relationship culture that will serve to bridge the two 'home' cultures and permit them to develop a working relationship.

A facilitating environment will depend on many factors and can only ever be regarded as a 'good enough' environment. However, there are certain principles that can be followed that will result in the sort of environment that will encourage the development of a healthy relationship. A facilitating environment is first absolutely, and then relatively, important, and the course of development can be described in terms of absolute dependence, relative dependence, and towards independence. For the infant and, it is postulated, for the parties of a relationship, the quality of the holding environment is vital. There is a need to develop a sense of security where they will carry around an expectation that they will not be 'let down'. In the holding environment developed by the parties to the relationship, the quality of conditions needs to be the same as in the maternal holding environment if it is to be regarded as a 'facilitating environment', that is, one which is healthy in the sense of there being maturity: one in which there will be progression. If all parties are to express themselves in a creative, spontaneous way, if they are not to be overwhelmed by anxiety, and if they are to have the confidence to overcome setbacks and still pursue their desires, they need to accept the responsibility for ensuring and developing a facilitating environment.

If we take the typical example of an interdepartmental meeting where heads of departments meet to agree resource allocation in the light of organizational objectives, we may see some of the possible problems with developing a good enough environment. Each head of department will almost certainly go to the meeting with the internalized projections of their staff pressuring them to get the best level of resources they can achieve. Each head of department will also go to the meeting with internalized experiences of the past behaviour of other heads of department, some of which may be positive and others negative. They may also go to the meeting with all sorts of other internalized experiences, including those from outside the organization. If there is to be a good, trusting, working relationship between the heads of department most of the negative experiences will need to be minimized before the meeting. A departmental head who is self-reflective and sufficiently self-aware will be capable of doing so.

Both or all parties have an important role to play if there is to be an environment where there is sufficient trust to allow all to begin to satisfy their needs for self-esteem by participating in the planning, organizing, and controlling of their own tasks. The various needs of individuals, such as growth, belonging, self-esteem, recognition, and self-actualization, can only be met where there is a mature situation. That is, a situation where individuals are able to be themselves and to understand and experience other people as distinct individuals who are separate and perhaps different from themselves and to be able to take part in co-operative relationships with these differentiated others. It is the role of both parties to ensure that such a mature situation exists.

Sadly, as is frequently the response in these circumstances, rather than try to develop a strategy for changing fundamental attitudes and practices in order to achieve the conditions for progression, the more typical approach by one or both parties is to seek more leverage for their power based, paternalistic tactics of bargaining, manipulation, intimidation, deception, legalistic manoeuvring, brinkmanship, conciliation, defamation, capitulation, and appeasement. As we will be aware, we all have a strong proclivity to turn difference into polarization. As human beings, if we need to feel good we need to see the other as bad. The problem is that we may respond in like manner. Of course, these tactics only serve to reinforce the lack of basic trust and make the prospects of developing co-operative relations even more remote. The result is an immature situation where there is little chance if any of progression.

As happens in any relationship, the real problem arises when we feel ourselves threatened but have little control

141

over the activities posing the threat. It is when we feel we cannot influence the most important things that happen to us, when they seem to follow the dictates of some inexorable power, that we give up trying to learn how to act on, or change them. We can perhaps try to imagine what it is like for an infant who is hungry, alone, or cold, and in spite of his or her crying and gestures there is no response. Being utterly dependent on mother for this care the infant must feel that he or she is totally impotent and experience this as some fearful dread. In similar manner, there is the danger that in any relationship there is a constant possibility that one or both parties will feel threatened and out of control.

In the most general sense, task satisfaction is a pleasurable or positive emotional state resulting from the appraisal of one's task experiences. This positive assessment or feeling seems to occur when the task is congruent with the individual's needs and values. In these circumstances the proclivity we evoke is the early relation with mother, the complementarity of the pair. Where there is no such congruence, where our values and needs do not match our task, there is a high likelihood that we will not only experience dissatisfaction but perhaps disaffection as well. Given such circumstances, trust will not exist and the relationship will suffer.

Returning to the above example of the heads of department meeting; where a head of department feels that they have fully participated and that the department view has been heard and considered, it will almost certainly be regarded as a positive co-operative experience. However, where the head of department feels that the meeting has been a 'stitch-up', and decisions predetermined by one or more members, he or she may, like a child, feel impotent, threatened, and not in control. In such circumstances any trust that previously existed will have gone and may take a very long time to be renewed.

Developing trust – hope, optimism, and confidence

A basic need of all concerned in any relationship is for 'esteem' – both self-esteem and recognition from others. Most people have a need for a high evaluation of themselves that is firmly based on reality – recognition and respect from others; especially significant others. We are in constant need of reassurance, although the same time sense that makes it possible for us to worry about what may happen also makes it possible to postpone the satisfaction of present needs and put up with current discomforts in the expectation of future rewards. This is a state of mind that we refer to as hope. Hope offers more than a bit of comfort in an anxiety-ridden world; it plays a surprisingly potent role in life, offering an advantage in realms as diverse as school achievement and bearing up in onerous jobs. It is more than the sunny view that everything will turn out all right. It is a belief that you have both the will and the way to accomplish your goals, whatever they may be.

As with hope, optimism is a state of mind that means having a strong expectation that, in general, things will turn out all right in life, despite setbacks and frustrations. Optimism is an attitude that helps us to avoid falling into apathy, hopelessness, or depression in the face of tough going. While the pessimistic individual's feelings lead to despair, the optimistic individual's feelings will be bright and hopeful. Where individuals have a high evaluation of themselves – a high self-esteem – they will have the self-belief that they have mastery over the events of their lives and can meet challenges as they come up. Whether we are

143

an optimist or a pessimist will be affected by our previous experiences. When an infant seeks attention and receives a prompt and satisfying response they may develop an optimistic view of life. When an infant's needs are left ignored or not satisfied they may develop a pessimistic view of life.

Another basic need is a desire for competence. Competence implies control over environmental factors, both physical and social. People with this motive do not wish to wait passively for things to happen; they want to be able to manipulate their environment and make things happen. The competence motive reveals itself in adults as a desire for job mastery and professional growth. Developing a competency of any kind strengthens the sense of self-esteem, making an individual more willing to take risks and seek out more demanding challenges. Those who have a high evaluation of themselves are able to bounce back from failures; they approach things in terms of how to handle them rather than worrying about what can go wrong.

By providing an organizational environment that encourages hope, optimism, and competence we shall be providing conditions that will also encourage trust. The departmental head who, as a result of his or her experience feels hopeful and optimistic, not only feels good about him or herself but also develops positive feelings about the complementarity of the relationships in the meeting. Such positive feelings will serve to encourage trust in those concerned.

Developing trust – containment

A facilitating environment will ensure that the anxiety of venturing into the unknown, the process by which individuals develop new skills and ways of behaving, is contained so that processes they are involved in are not fundamentally disruptive. Any change will involve a loss; it will mean a change from the comfortable, routine, known way of doing things. A giving up of things is taken for granted. All change will result in some level of anxiety. Where the right sort of environment exists the anxiety can be dominated just because the thread of continuity has not been broken and can always be given a reassuring tug. Spontaneous growth follows from the consolidation of familiar patterns of expectation. A facilitating environment will provide the consistency, confirmation, and continuity that helps the parties to a relationship make sense of their world: it will both hold them and let go of them.

Continuing with the example of our head of department, the meeting may not develop as expected. Unexpected occurrences may have changed the purpose of the meeting from one of allocation of resources to that of reduction of resources. For our head of department this may come as something of a shock and create considerable anxiety as to the likely implications and the problems associated with informing the department staff. If the relationship in the meeting has previously been experienced as complementary and trusting, they will all be able to work co-operatively to find a solution. However, where trust has not previously existed there may be harmful competition and protection of boundaries as a result of the anxiety.

When a party to the relationship offers security they do two things at once. On the one hand, because of their help other individuals feel they are safe from the unexpected, from innumerable unwelcome intrusions, and from a world that is at times not known or understood. On the other hand, other individuals are protected by their actions from their own impulses and from the effects that these impulses might produce. For example, providing support and encouragement to others even when they are experiencing what may be regarded as the 'most rotten luck', will shield them and keep them in touch with reality. It will also protect them from their impulses to phantasize that there is a jinx on them, or something of the sort.

If we are to provide support and encouragement to others we first need to be capable of self-awareness so that we can control and mange our own feelings. In doing so we remain in touch with reality for longer periods and are less likely to engage in phantasy. If we return for a moment to the head of department, if he is a reflective manager who has an awareness of beneath-the-surface processes, he may be able to identify these when they occur in others and positively work at shielding them by keeping in touch with reality.

Perhaps the most outstanding and most continuously operative needs of all relationships is that for emotional response from the other party. I use the term emotional response advisedly, since the eliciting of mere behavioural responses may leave this need quite unsatisfied. We all know what it's like to be alone in a crowd, and we all know what it's like to be dealt with by someone who is acting like a 'cold fish'. It is this need for a response, and especially for praise, that provides individuals with their main stimulus to socially acceptable behaviour. One of the reasons why parties to a relationship may abide by the values of the relationship is because they desire approval. If we are to encourage trust in any relationship, communication at

146

an emotional level, especially empathy, is the most vital and essential element. If we try to create an environment that is evidenced by hope, optimism, and competence, this will be beneficial. But without communication at an emotional level trust is unlikely to positively develop.

As was my intention, this Section has exposed and explored some of the dynamics occurring beneath the surface in regard to relationships. Reflecting on the material I am amazed by the complexity of learning about the interpersonal level of political activity. And I have the feeling of being totally inadequate in not being able to provide an exposure and exploration of all that is likely to occur. However, I am also well aware that human beings make meaning out of complexity at every moment of their waking, and sleeping, lives. But this only serves to leave me feeling humbled by the thought that what others do so naturally in their everyday lives I have the greatest difficulty in doing in a few pages. Perhaps, though, this may give us a clue as to why we sometimes prefer to take things at their face value.

9. Towards groups

As if the world were not complicated enough, we don't live in a world of individuals and relationships; from birth onwards we are constantly members of groups and these require and will have further exposure and exploration in the next Section. It is fair to say that all beneath-the-surface activity exposed and explored thus far is equally applicable to groups. Virtually everything contained in the Preface and Sections One and Two directly applies to group dynamics. In some instances they will be derivatives of individual dynamics and in other instances they may be seen as an extension of individual relationships to relations between groups and individuals or between groups and groups.

Of central theoretical and practical interest to a reflective approach is what I have termed 'relatedness': the process of mutual influence between individual and group, group and group, and group and organization. And we might go beyond this to consider the relatedness of organization and community to wider social systems, to society itself, as we shall see in Section Three. In all these forms of relatedness there is a potential tension. As individuals we need groups in order to establish our identity, to find meaning in our existence, and to express different aspects of ourselves. Correspondingly, the group also needs the individual member for its own collective purposes – both to contribute to the group's task and also to participate in the processes through which the group acquires and maintains its own distinctive identity. But this process is one that often threatens individuality.

SECTION THREE

Groups

In this Section the focus is on groups. As in the preceding two Sections the intention is to go beyond taking things at their face value by going deeper and exploring the underlying, less evident phenomena concerning groups that occur beneath the surface. The more frequently used approach is to study the behaviour of the individuals in a group. This is one way of creating an understanding of group behaviour. However, the approach taken here is to study groups from the perspective of the group-as-a-whole. In doing so, we can identify and understand other important behaviour that will provide a totally different perspective. Thus, while individual actions and relationships in groups is a valid field of study, there is this other level, the group-as-a-whole, which becomes the unit of study from the group level perspective.

We may speak, for convenience, about the individual and the group, but in practice these two can never be separated and should not be considered even theoretically in isolation. Physical assembly of people into a group simply makes 'political' characteristics of human beings more easily demonstrable. In reality, none of us, however isolated in time and space, can be regarded as outside a group or lacking in active manifestations of group psychology. We carry our groupishness with us all the time and it is clear that everything is embedded in the social context of our lives, particularly in the dominant primary group, the family. As will be shown, the behaviour observed in groups is not to be considered a product of groups as such but of the fact that the 'human being is a group animal'.

The group-as-a-whole is a level of analysis that represents processes that may be more or less than the sum of the individual members of the group and their interpersonal dynamics. The group-as-a-whole can be conceptualized as behaving in a different manner from, but related to, the dynamics of the members. From this vantage point groups-as-a-whole have their own dynamics resulting from the interactions of group members who are interdependent members and sub-systems. In effect, the group becomes a thing, it is reified 'as if' a group mind exists, and it is experienced as being as real as an individual's brain in which thinking and feeling occur. Throughout this Section I expose and explore the way that mainly unconscious dynamics beneath the surface of groups are as important as those concerning individuals.

Some of the beneath-the-surface dynamics that occur in groups and organizations are similar to those described in Section One. In particular, the ways that we as individuals develop defences as a means of avoiding and defending against anxiety. Albeit in a slightly different manner, these are replicated in groups and organizations. As you will discover, this is not surprising, as groups evoke feelings associated with the maternal holding environment, so that, when members of groups experience frustration and anxiety, they are likely to respond by using primitive processes as they did in childhood. At a group level these defences result in important phenomena that will be described and referred to as social systems as a defence against anxiety.

1. The group-as-a-whole

The focus of this Section is on groups, but that does not mean that we should ignore the beneath-the-surface processes that have been exposed in the last two Sections. Virtually all that has been referred to regarding individuals and relationships is equally applicable to groups. And it may be helpful for the reader to bear in mind the way that we use beneath-the-surface processes to make sense of our world and to help us deal with unbearable thoughts and feelings. This Section will build on this knowledge by exposing and exploring some of the beneath-the-surface processes that are exclusive to groups.

We will probably all be familiar with the notion that the performance of a team is superior to the individual efforts of the members: that the sum is greater than the parts. This is a helpful starting position in beginning to understand something of the dynamics concerned. What though, we might ask, is this team or group? We will also be familiar with frequent references to the notion of a group mind, or of groups behaving as an organism. Indeed, it is not uncommon for some to erroneously speak of organizations as actively doing something or other. Again, we may ask, how can this be? We know that only individuals have minds and that no such thing as a group mind exists. It is individual human beings who are constantly engaged in the process of meaning-making. Or, to put it as previously stated, it is not about the doing that a human does, it is about the doing that a human is. How or why, then, do we develop the idea that a 'group mind' exists?

What we can say is that groups act 'as if' they have a group mind. But you may well say that this still poses the question, how does this come about? Clearly, individuals must be involved in making sense of their surrounding experience, and it must, therefore, be individuals who are concerned with the development of this phenomenon that resembles a group mind. We will recall that there is no feeling, no experience, no thought, no perception independent of a meaning-making context in which it becomes a feeling, an experience, a thought, a perception, because we are the meaning-making context. If the members of a group, as human beings, did not take in their various sensations and translate them into something they would not be what they are. It would seem, then, that the group is a construct and that without individual human activity the construct of the group-as-a-whole simply would not exist.

Developing the construct: group-as-a-whole

In seeking an explanation that will enable us to understand how the vitally important construct of a group-as-a-whole comes about, we need once again to return to the earliest days of human existence. The reader may need little reminding that, when born, the infant is totally dependent on his or her mother for both psychological and social support. The mother provides what might helpfully be referred to as a maternal holding environment. Holding in the mother's womb and then holding in the mother's arms is the first boundary out of chaos within which the infant's personality can develop. The early relation in the maternal holding environment is characterized by infantile dependence; that is, a dependence based on a primary identification with the object, and an inability to differentiate and adapt.

The need for attachment to the mother is such that individuals are so completely dependent on others during infancy that they cannot survive without eliciting responses from their parents or other carers. As was explained in Section Two, the infant's journey from dependency to separation is somewhat of a struggle, and it would appear that the infant is involved in a series of repeated separations from and reunions with the mother. Each step of psychological independence is welcomed for the sense of freedom but feared for the threat of abandonment, isolation, and loss of object love. We are never totally independent even after 'me' and 'not me' have been established. Perhaps, then, it is not surprising that this experience stays with us and is so influential throughout our lives. Deep in our unconscious is a strong and impenetrable bond with our mother that lasts forever and there is always a danger of regressing to the comfortable dependent position. Such was that experience that none of us dares to give up our inborn need for maternal gratification. None of us is truly independent, even in adult life, and from time to time we cling to each other as if we are mothers to each other.

The individual is part of a group from earliest infancy, initially a group of two, the mother–infant dyad, then a group of three or more as the existence of father and siblings have to be accommodated, and later a series of overlapping family and social groups. These co-exist in external reality and in the developing of the individual's internal world. A result is the development of that which I shall refer to as 'groupishness', and the need and yearning for the 'good' mother that are believed to reside in the very core of our being. This is connected to the need for a favourable emotional response from the mother that was described as being necessary for the well-being or very existence of the infant. As a result of these processes it is thus that the group entity can become for the individual the symbolic representation of a nurturing mother.

Influence of maternal holding environment

Being a member of a group will trigger unconscious feelings associated with our early and highly potent emotional maternal bond, so that we are not only reminded of that situation but treat the group as if it were the maternal holding environment. Terms such as 'mother earth' and 'motherland', or even Alma Mater, which are used popularly, are of relevance here. In a broader sense the hypothesis can be advanced that our human need to belong and to establish a state of psychological unity with others represents a covert wish for restoring an earlier state of unconflicted well-being inherent in the exclusive union with mother. Put another way, we seek to recreate in the present day group a holding environment that will provide us with the same sort of psychological and social support we experienced in the maternal holding environment.

As discussed in Section One, a result of our individual ability to form concepts means that we can construct an object in the mind that is a non-human object. The group is to be seen as such an artificial creation; it is a mental construct. More than this, though, it is a mental construct that develops out of our internalized pool of knowledge and feelings of the maternal holding environment. Thus, the construct that is 'group' becomes the nurturing mother that we unconsciously feel will provide the psychological and social support previously experienced. We need the group to provide us with a favourable emotional response as much as we needed mother to do so. A measure of the importance that the group has for us is perhaps illustrated by the way we quickly come to identify with a group.

Any of us who have experienced the process of joining a group, even in a temporary situation, will reflect how this became 'our' group and that this group took on a form of identity for us. Our group also had boundaries that determined who was a member of that group and who was not. Having created the construct of a group or organization it is reified, and the members of the group act 'as if' it exists and, because of our experience, even if the object is not human, it is associated with human activity. A result is that we therefore attach to this object the same attributes as other influential objects, especially the mother. We attach to the group (held in the mind) the same emotions, so that, to a lesser or greater degree, the members of a group will experience the same feelings. We sometimes get an indication of this when members of an organization speak of it as 'not caring', or of it being a 'really caring organization'.

At its core, the group-as-a-whole perspective is derived from the notion that conceptually treats the construct that is the 'group in the mind' as being similar to, and for the members of groups reacting to the concept 'as if' it were, the construct 'mother in the mind'. As previously discussed, out of the totality of our early experience through the process of introjection the infant creates a construct that is 'mother in the mind'. 'My Mum' is the infant's view of mother as seen by the infant. This view of mother in the mind affects the way the infant behaves because he or she wishes to please mother and not to make her angry, as, at this stage, she is the source of all pleasure. Individual behaviour in groups is seen to equate with the unconscious reactions and manoeuvres of infants in relation to the ambivalently held mothering object. Consequently, we might well anticipate that the group in the mind will also affect the way group members behave, because they will view the group as the source of all pleasure. We may also expect that when members of groups experience frustration and anxiety they are likely to respond by using primitive processes such as splitting, projection, and introjection.

Since all individuals go through the experiences of infancy, we can be sure that the most outstanding and most continuous of human psychic needs is that of emotional response from other individuals. We will recall that the individual is so completely dependent at this stage that he or she cannot survive without eliciting emotional responses from mother. Attachment is a deep and universal need and we all know what it means to be alone in a crowd. In adult life it is this need for a response, and especially for a favourable response, which provides individuals with their main stimulus to socially acceptable behaviour. People abide by the mores of their groups and societies quite as much because they desire approval as because they fear punishment. The way that members of a group unconsciously treat the group as the maternal holding environment is because the need for attachment is so strong. This will, in turn have the effect of achieving greater and closer 'groupishness', by which process a number of individuals unconsciously develop the concept of being one, of being a group.

Influence of regression

But this may not provide a full explanation. The individual's very belief that a group exists as a separate entity can be seen as regression. Regression to a state where, to put it crudely, the group is mother, but before mother was

157

experienced as a person entirely distinct from other significant members of the family constellation and before that
'other' was clearly established. As with the infant relating
to the mother, the adult must establish contact with the
emotional life of the group in which he or she lives. This
task would appear to be as formidable to the adult as the
relationship with the breast appears to be to the infant,
and the failure to meet the demands of this task is revealed
in his or her regression. The creation of the concept of the
'group in the mind' and the subsequent belief that a group
exists, as distinct from an aggregate of individuals, is an
essential part of the regression.

The group as mother analogy fundamentally draws the
parallels between infant in relation to mother and individual in relation to group. The central thrust here is that
the group situation creates such ambivalence and anxiety
that it unconsciously returns the group members to earlier
relationships with mother and evokes all of the psychosocial mechanisms involved. In sum, groups, in a similar
manner to the mothering object, create strong, conflicting, ambivalent feelings of love and hate, bliss and despair,
dread and joy. Primitive ambivalence, anxiety, and regression are generated as a consequence of the fact that the
group represents the primal mother. The natural psychological habitat of man is the group, but man's adaptation
to that habitat is imperfect, a state of affairs that is
reflected in his chronic ambivalence towards groups.
Group membership is psychologically essential and yet a
source of increasing discomfort.

Influence of identification

A further explanation may lie in the notion of identification. Identification brings into play such functions as

adaptation to reality, reality testing, a sense of reality, the self concept (with its self and object relations), and the capacity to form object relationships. Questions such as, Who am I? Where have I been? Where am I going? are deeply ensconced in the individual's group experiences from the family on and out. Since most human needs are supplied by other persons, adaptation to the world is with the world of other people and not with the world of nature. This provides a further impetus for our 'groupishness'. Members of a group test reality by comparing their own perceptions and evaluations with those of other group members who experience the same or similar events. The 'truth' of reality concepts is developed in the bubbling cauldron of consensus, not in the isolation of lonely contemplation. Members of groups test reality by comparing their perceptions and evaluations with those of other persons who experience the same or similar experiences. This may result in shared qualities, interests, or ideals being capable of precipitating identifications with others or identification as an emotional tie between people. In this way reality testing – the need for consistency, continuity, and confirmation – may lead to consensual validation.

Identification with a group in the mind goes beyond the mere perception of it and the investing of it with some emotional element for identification in this sense also contains an element of responding or more specifically, an element of individual commitment. The result of an individual's group identification is that he or she reacts to the attributes of the group as if these attributes were also his or hers. A striking illustration is the way an individual reacts to a criticism or slight of his group as if he himself had been criticized or slighted. To belong to, or to feel part of, a group also implies a more or less transient giving up of some aspect of the individual's self to the group as a group.

As for identification with the group-as-a-whole, the process can perhaps be best explored within the framework of the individual group member's perception. At any moment of his or her group membership each individual can be said to perceive selected aspects of an existing social situation. That may include interacting with group members and a central person or persons, but also the group-as-a-whole. As a result of identification with the group-as-a-whole the group is no longer viewed through its individual components, rather, the group holding environment is seen 'as if' it were an organism – an entity in its own right, possessing dynamics, structures, and development independent of and reaching beyond the individuals who make it up. To the extent that the focus is on the individual, he is to be viewed as a representative of the group for which he stands, and in turn the manner in which he is treated represents relatedness to this entire group.

Influence of relatedness

Of central theoretical and practical interest to groups is what I have termed 'relatedness': the process of mutual influence between individual and group, group and group, and group and organization. Furthermore, we might go beyond this to consider the relatedness of organization and community to wider social systems, to society itself. In all these forms of relatedness there is a potential tension. The individual needs groups in order to establish their identity, to find meaning in their existence, and to express different aspects of themselves.

Correspondingly, the group also needs the individual member for its own collective purposes – both to contribute to the group's task and also to participate in the processes through which the group acquires and maintains its own distinctive identity. This provides a further impetus for our 'groupishness', but this process is one that often threatens individuality.

The group being viewed as a whole, as an organism or an entity in its own right that possesses dynamics, structure, and development independent of the individual, has the effect of reducing the individual to being part of the whole. The individual is but a component element of the group who may be viewed as being representative of the group and acting on behalf of the group. Freud took notice of individual behaviour only so far as it was expressive of developments in the group-as-a-whole. That is to say, if a group member attacked the leader, he would attempt to interpret why this was being done on behalf of the group at a given moment – neglecting, although he was fully aware of the fact, that this behaviour was also meaningful to the individual in the light of his own particular history. To put it another way, we take the object of analysis to be all the evidence produced by group members that we believe belongs to a group: the common fantasies, the concerted behaviours and tacit agreements that point to the existence of a shared group mentality. Thus, we are concerned with the way that an individual is mobilized by the group to do something on their behalf; there is an assumption that individuals are speaking on behalf of the group and not as individuals; they are representing the group.

An example may concern a workplace meeting of an organizational group where the item under discussion is provoking considerable anxiety. The discussion and debate around the issue is going nowhere and the members of the group are becoming increasingly angry and frustrated as a result of the predicament in which they find themselves. At some point one of the group members leads them in a discussion about an unrelated topic that other group members willingly join to. In doing so the individual has led them away from the anxiety-provoking task on to a meaningless but safe discussion. At the face value level, we may say that the individual got fed up and decided to change the subject matter. But at the level of the group-as-a-whole, we will view this as the individual being mobilized by the group to do something on their behalf. In this instance the individual was mobilized as a flight leader who would, through this beneath-the-surface process, help them to avoid their anxiety.

Individuals and sub-group roles as function of group-as-a-whole

Our primary focus in groups needs to be the group-as-a-whole and this includes what individuals or sub-groups may do. Roles that are taken up by group members are a function of the group-as-a-whole and the behaviour of a person in a group has more to do with the group than it does with his individuality. I should stress that I am not here referring to formal, allocated roles, but to roles that members of a group unconsciously take on as a result of beneath-the-surface processes. In other words, any role taken by an individual member of a group may be considered to be a group role, one that is a function of group dynamics. When role is defined as a property of the group, then role prescriptions are filled, sometimes by individuals, sometimes by sub-groups, and sometimes by identifiable clusters of behaviour that are a group property and serve a group role function, although they appear independent from all individual members or sub-groups. These group role dynamics are to be seen as a manifestation of the group-as-a-whole.

An example might be the way a group of women might represent an unconscious dynamic in a group concerning a perceived or actual gender conflict within the group. At the surface level, in terms of what was being discussed in the group, there might be little if any indication of the unconscious processes that were occurring. But at a beneath-the-surface level the unconscious formation and clustering of the women may be seen as a response to the underlying dynamics. By physically and psychologically coming together they may be defending against an unconsciously perceived attack by the men in the group. At some point in the process this unconscious activity may be triggered into conscious activity. Here we can see how the sum of the group-as-a-whole is different from the individual group members.

Group processes are indeed different from individual dynamics and specific group dynamics occur that are of a different nature than individual dynamics, albeit that they have their origins in the individual. The group-as-a-whole is a level of analysis that represents processes that may be more or less than the sum of the individual members of the group and their interpersonal dynamics. The group-as-a-whole can be conceptualized as behaving in a different manner from, but related to, the dynamics of the members. From this vantage point groups-as-a-whole have their own dynamics resulting from the interactions of group members who may be seen as interdependent members and subsystems. Thus, while the individual actions and relationships is a valid field of study, there is this other level, the group-as-a-whole, which becomes the unit of study from the group level perspective.

The behaviour observed in groups is not a product of groups as such but of the fact that the 'human being is a group animal'. We carry our groupishness with us all the time. Physical assembly of people into a group simply makes 'political' characteristics of human beings more easily demonstrable. However, physical assembly is not a prerequisite for the existence of a group. No individual, however isolated in time and space, can be regarded as outside a group or lacking in active manifestations of group psychology. Take for example, a group of personnel managers who are located in disparate parts of a large organization. They seldom, if ever, come together physically, but they are still very much a group in the mind for those concerned. In like manner, a family may no longer be part of the same physical home or even be in the same town or same country, but they will still regard themselves as a family group regardless of how often they may be together physically. Both the family and the personnel managers are not only part of a group in the mind but are very much related to each other in a mutually influential way.

To put the foregoing in some sort of context I wish to make it clear that I am talking about any sort of group or organization. All beneath-the-surface activity referred to will have an effect on every single group because that's what a group is; and that's what a group does. To summarize, the group-as-a-whole phenomenon assumes that individuals and sub-groups are vehicles that reflect and express the group-as-a-whole. Individual group members are acting together unconsciously as a collusive whole in which their interactions and shared fantasies create and represent at once the group-as-a-whole. It is from this premise that an individual speaking or acting in a group is perceived as expressing aspects of the group. This is so whether we are referring to a family group, a residents' group, a small group with responsibility for a particular task in an organization, a whole department, or an entire organization. Each group will be unique and continuing experiences will be unique. The unique features of each group will be part of the consideration as to how it is experienced.

An important group-as-a-whole dynamic is culture, which is explored in the next sub-section. This explanation of culture will provide a continuation of, and will enable us to add to our understanding of, the notion of group-as-a-whole.

2. Culture

The term 'culture' has been in common usage for many years and is a familiar notion. Unfortunately, this common usage has itself led to problems. For example, cultural differences are seen as being in the nature of things requiring no explanation. A result is that functions that are not easily understood are assigned to a mysterious central agency called 'culture', accompanied by a declaration that 'it' performs in a particular way. Culture is also an easy option to fall back on to solve all our unexplained problems. In addition, past uses of the word to designate a way of life such as a particular society, or part of a society, are exceedingly vague.

However, as vague as our understanding of culture may be, it is also vital to our understanding of different orga-

nizations and societies and in particular to our understanding of cross-cultural relationships. Organizational
and societal culture are complicated yet highly influential
phenomena and the degree of complication is likely to be
much greater in a situation where multiple societal
cultures prevail. Some parts of the social sciences, such as
anthropology and sociology, tend to base their object of
study on patterns of social behaviour and do not recognize that individuals and psychology are also involved in
the processes of culture. I believe that this has led to a situation where we have been more concerned with identifying the symptoms of a culture than with understanding
what it is.

The approach taken here seeks to provide an answer to
that most fundamental of questions: that concerning how
culture develops. In doing so I shall be working from the
principle that if we know how it develops then we shall be
able to unpack it and therefore know how to influence it.
In other words, knowing how culture develops will
provide us with an understanding of the causes of the
consistent behaviour that we call culture. So, what is it
that we are we trying to understand? In simple terms, we
are trying to understand processes of human behaviour
that by their very nature are dynamic; that is, they exist in
a state of flux and are characterized by spontaneity, freedom, experience, conflict, and movement.

The constant interaction between the individual and
culture is fundamental to any study of culture or, for that
matter, personality. They are indivisibly linked and consequently it will be necessary to refer to both processes.
Indeed, we may take as our first premise the notion that
the function of the personality as a whole is to enable the
individual to produce forms of behaviour that they feel

166

will be psychologically advantageous to them under the conditions that they perceive are imposed on them by their environment. Put another way, it is a social psychology.

Organizational culture

In brief, we can say that culture may be characterized by the following:

1. It is a psycho-social process that develops out of the interrelatedness of the members of a group or organization with the group or organizational holding environment.
2. It is evidenced by sameness and continuity to provide for the self-esteem of the members and their sense of reality with others.
3. Being a psychological as well as a social process it is influenced by conscious and unconscious processes.
4. Both the uniqueness of the collective, perceived view of the members of the organization and the organizational holding environment results in a unique culture in every organization and part of an organization.
5. Because groups are ongoing structures as opposed to finished ones, it is a dynamic and changing process.
6. The members of a group, organization, or society will produce forms of behaviour that will be psychologically advantageous to them under the conditions imposed by the environment.

The influences which societal culture exerts on the developing personality are of two quite different sorts. On the one hand, we have those influences that derive from the culturally patterned behaviour of individuals towards the child. What might be described as the socially accepted

167

processes of mothering and parenting begins to operate from the moment of birth. On the other hand, we have those influences that derive from the individual's observation of, or instruction in, the patterns of behaviour characteristic of their society. Out of the relatedness of the mother and infant develops a mutual influence on the personality. The fact that personality norms differ in different societies can be explained on the basis of the different experiences that the members of such societies acquire from contact with those societies. However, what we need to study is the processes of these societal experiences.

Influence of maternal holding environment

Every society consists of individuals developing from children into parents. In the earliest days the mother provides the context in which development takes place, and from the point of view of the new-born she is part of the self. She provides a true psycho-social context: she is both 'psycho' and 'social' depending on whose perspective we take, and the transformation by which she becomes for the infant gradually less 'psycho' and more 'social' describes the very evolution of meaning itself. What we have referred to as the 'maternal holding environment' is vital to the development of the infant. From the beginning of life, reliable holding has to be a feature of the environment if the child is to survive.

The notion of a 'holding environment' is seen as the key concept in providing an explanation of how culture develops. The dynamics and processes concerned in the development of the maternal holding environment have been widely referred to earlier in the book. But, in brief we may describe the process as follows: The 'maternal holding environment' consists first of the mother and child and later the father and other important relatives. In this 'holding environment' there is a continuing interrelationship between the mother and the child. The mother influences the child and the child influences the mother. In other words, the child is part of the 'holding environment' and influences it while at the same time the child is influenced by the 'holding environment'. The maternal holding environment is not a closed system but is also open to external influences, such as, for example, noise or changes in temperature. The development of the personality of the child will depend upon whether the holding environment has been 'good enough'.

Building on the concept of a 'maternal holding environment', the growing infant becomes a member of several holding environments; the family, the school, the university, the organizational or work, and the societal holding environments. Indeed, I will go further than this, because I believe it is more accurate to state that there is not only a succession of 'holding environments' but that several 'holding environments' may be available for any one individual at any given time. This may be especially so regarding societal, work, and family holding environments, which we will all influence and at the same time be influenced by. All these holding environments will be experienced by the individual members as a group-as-a-whole. On becoming a member of, say, a school group or a work group, the individual member will unconsciously experience the group as if it were the maternal holding environment.

Organizational holding environment

Having demonstrated the importance of the maternal holding environment in the process of the development of

169

personality, I shall now develop the concept of an 'organizational holding environment'. It is my contention that in a similar manner to the relationship of the individual with his or her maternal holding environment, the organization also becomes a partly conscious and partly unconscious holding environment for its members. As part of the organizational holding environment – and in common with the maternal holding environment – we each influence the organizations we are in and they influence us and our behaviour. But, of course, the reader will appreciate that, unlike the maternal holding environment, there is no actual 'mother' in the organization setting. Essentially, as was discussed above, what happens is that we identify with the organization 'as if' it were real. It is what we might refer to as an 'organization held in the mind'. It is a construct that we identify with and treat 'as if' it were real.

In much the same way that we interrelate with the maternal holding environment, so we also interrelate with the organization holding environment. We use it to supply the same needs as the maternal holding environment and we apply the same emotion to it and create similar defences when it is seen as 'not good enough'. We are never totally independent, the healthy individual does not become isolated, but continues to be related to the environment, or part of the environment, such as an organization, in such a way that the individual and the environment can be said to be interdependent. Because we psychologically treat this holding environment as if it were the maternal holding environment we still look to it to provide for our social and psychological well-being. In much the same way as there is a need for a 'basic trust' in the maternal holding environment and for what has been termed a 'good enough holding environment', so there is a similar need here in regard to the organization holding environment. As with the mother, such 'basic trust' is developed as a result of the perceived experience of the organization holding environment by the members of the organization.

The same sort of unconscious forces that operate in the maternal holding environment are also operating here in the organizational holding environment. As has been explained, by the process of classification we continually add new experiences to our pool of internalized knowledge and feelings. This is, of course, equally true of experiences in groups and organizations where we may introject the object in the mind that is the group or organization and all the associated feelings that go with them. Seen as a totality, the group or organizational holding environment is a rather complex and difficult phenomenon to study. An approach that will lift the veil of understanding is to view human behaviour as a psycho-social process. The concept of 'psycho-social' draws attention to the fact that what we are dealing with in social systems is two distinct levels at the same time. That is, we need to conceptualize a group, an organization, or society as a process of human behaviour that is both psychological and social at the same time. To further expose and explore the processes involved it is helpful to separate internal and external parts of the holding environment and I will refer to these parts as the internal holding environment and the external holding environment.

The external holding environment

In this respect, the 'iceberg' analogy previously used by other writers may be a useful way of viewing things. The physical or sociological part of the holding environment is that part which is exposed or is conscious. This is the *external holding environment*, which consists of: the technological, economic, sociological, and political factors; the products and services the group, organization, or institution provides; and the organizational structures, strategies, and procedures that management or politicians have created that together comprise the everyday life of the organization or institution. Those aspects of the processes of human behaviour may be regarded as the 'external' realities of the members of the organization. These are the rational aspects of organizations and these are what we have referred to as 'knowing about'. This level is frequently the full extent of our knowledge and understanding – the rational and seemingly predictable aspects of human behaviour. But, of course, that's not all there is to human behaviour. As well as the social level we also need to consider the ever-present psychological level of human behaviour.

The internal holding environment

The psychological part of the holding environment is the concealed, beneath-the-surface, internalized and largely unconscious part. This is *the internalized holding environment* that consists of the subjective experience of members of a group, organization or institution: about what goes on in the minds of members of the group, organization, or society. This may include the ideas and ways of thinking about how they perceive the external realities in relation to how they behave or act. Their actions will be influenced by their beliefs, values, hopes, anxieties, and the defence mechanisms that they employ. Put another way, we are referring to the 'internal' realities of the members of the organization. These are the irrational and unconscious aspects of us all and these are influenced by what we have referred to as 'knowledge of experience'.

These two levels, the external and internal worlds of people – are in continual interaction. It will be recalled that we make meaning out of our experiences, and experience itself is at the boundary between the two worlds – external interaction and internal interpretation. We experience the group, organization, or institutional holding environment through our perceptive processes and filter them down and match them against our pool of internalized knowledge and feelings consisting of our past experience. In this way, the subjective processes of the members of the group, organization, or institution affect the way they determine reality. Each experience will be shaped by the group or organizational member's previous experience.

Culture develops out of the interrelatedness of the members of the organization and the organizational holding environment. The organizational holding environment consists of the totality of the organization, including the members of the organization themselves. The specific organization holding environment provides the context in which development of culture takes place. If the organization is to work towards its primary task there is a need for a social system that relates technology to task and relates the people and groups who carry out different parts of the task to each other. Task, structure, and technology, which are part of the external holding environment, will not in themselves account for the nature of the social system, although they may put significant constraints on it.

The reader will be aware that, unlike other phenomena described in this book, I have not provided examples to help explain and describe the processes referred to. This is not an error but a simple recognition that it is not possible and that it would not be helpful to do so. Providing an example would simply be a description of a symptom of a culture rather than culture itself. In this regard there are two points about culture that I would wish to stress. The first point is that culture is something that an organization or institution 'is', as opposed to something an organization or institution 'has'. Culture is a group-as-a-whole dynamic pro-cess in the same way that personality is something that a person 'is'. It cannot be split off and examined, or changed, as some would have us believe. It develops out of the interrelatedness of the members of the organization and the organizational holding environment.

The second point is that every culture, like every personality, is unique. Each group, organization, or institution is unique and therefore each culture is unique. Consequently, to describe one culture would provide the reader with little if any helpful information about culture in other groups, organizations, or institutions. The way a culture develops may be affected by a multitude of options. To state but a few, we might start with the Managing Director. This person, who is a significant part of the external holding environment, may be perceived in all manner of ways: too soft or too hard; competent or incompetent; kind or uncaring; professional or unprofessional. Another significant part of the external holding environment is the formal strategy that may also be viewed in many different ways: relevant or irrelevant to today's market needs; to employee needs; to environmental needs; or to ethical needs. We could explore all aspects of the external holding environment and come up with a huge list of variables, such as those concerning the MD and strategy. But the thing we need to bear in mind is that for each group, organization, or institution the external holding environment and its component parts will be unique to that particular group, organization, or institution, as will be the members. Arising from the interrelatedness of the members and the holding environment will develop the construct that we refer to as the organization in the mind.

Our perceptions and experiences may consciously concern what is occurring at the physical or social level in the external holding environment. Here, various aspects may be regarded in a positive or negative manner. In each unique group or organizational holding environment there may be various aspects within that totality that will have a particular influence on the members' perceived notion of the organization in the mind. In the maternal holding environment, the particular influence was the mother and later the father and other important relatives. In the organizational holding environment it may be the Chief Executive, the ruling coalition or other significant figures; in others it may be the strategy (or lack of), or structure. These objects may arouse feelings of love or of hatred. What I would stress is that what is happening in the external holding environment will be the basis for the way the culture develops.

In regard to the internal holding environment, we will be concerned with beneath-the-surface processes. What goes on in the minds of people is partly reactive to what happens around them, but is also very much proactive. People's ideas and ways of thinking influence the way they act upon their surroundings to bring about change in them. This is all part and parcel of the dynamic processes. The biggest influence is likely to come from the internal

175

holding environment, and the social system that is developed is likely to reflect strongly the psychological and social satisfactions that members of an organization or institution seek in their membership and work in the organization or institution. These needs are of different kinds and are both positively task-orientated and potentially antitask. In so far as they are task-orientated they include the satisfactions arising from being able to deploy one self positively and fully in relation to task, co-operating effectively with others and experiencing both personal and organizational or institutional success in task performance.

Sentient groups

The latter is what we might refer to as a sentient group. That is, a group where the emotions and feelings are complementary to the task of the group. A sentient group is one which may result in loyalty to the organization from its members. It is a group towards which the individuals are prepared to commit themselves and on which they depend for emotional support. Whether or not individuals are prepared to work at the task and to give their all in the furtherance of the task will clearly depend on the sentience of the group. Psychological and social satisfactions are emotional experiences, if these are not satisfied, individuals may work to a different task.

In many instances the forms of behaviour adopted by the members of an organization will be aimed at and intended to be behaviour that is intended to achieve the primary task or intended purpose of the organization. In these instances the arrangements in the social or external holding environment will be in tune with the psychological or internal holding environment of the organization.

176

However, there are many reasons why the behaviour that members of the organization adopt as being appropriate to them is antitask. The likely result is that the way things are done around here is not appropriate to the performance of the primary task; it is more likely to be a culture that seeks to avoid the anxiety experienced by the members of the organization.

The need for a 'basic trust'

The way that the members of the organization perceive the 'organization in the mind' will determine the culture. It will depend on whether or not there is a 'basic trust' and whether the holding environment is viewed as 'good enough'. The behaviour adopted by the members of the organization will depend upon their psychological perception of the organization holding environment, or their view of the 'organization in their minds'. Whatever their view, members of the organization will adopt forms of behaviour that they feel are psychologically appropriate to them under the circumstances that they perceive are imposed upon them by their holding environment, whether this is task related or antitask behaviour. The end result is consistent forms of behaviour that have previously been defined as 'the way things are done around here'.

In a similar manner to the way that personality develops, so also will the way that culture develops depend upon the perceived experience of the organizational holding environment by the individual members of the organization. If they experience the manager or management as the kind of administrator or administration that provides sensitive care and a sense of trustworthiness within a trusted framework of their relationship, the members of the organization may adopt task-related forms of behaviour that they feel are psychologically advantageous to them under the circumstances imposed upon them by that environment.

Societal culture and its influence

All groups, organizations, and institutions are open systems and will be affected by societal dynamics. At this point, therefore, I shall briefly refer to societal dynamics. As has been demonstrated, the issue of organizational culture is complicated enough and we can start from the assumption that societal culture is somewhat more complicated, as there are even more influences than in the organizational setting. Individuals, as Freud so shrewdly observed, belong to many groups, have identifications in many directions and a variety of models upon which to build an ego ideal. Or, to put it as was stated earlier, we become members of several holding environments. We might see this as adding to the notion of multiple roles and multiple identities referred to in the last Section. And we might now consider the influence of political activity at the level of the international political system.

Complicated as it may be, by building on the approach outlined we can begin to make sense of societal culture. As with organizations we can say that societal culture develops out of the interrelatedness of the members of society and the societal holding environment. Starting from the notion of a societal holding environment we can begin to unpack societal culture and to establish how it has developed. As with organizational culture we can again view the societal holding environment as consisting of an internalized psychological part and an external social and physical part.

Societal external holding environment

The external holding environment will consist, among other things, of significant leaders such as the Prime Minister and the Queen in Britain; the government and the policies and structures that they adopt; local government and the policies and structures that they adopt; and, the media. In the most general of terms, these are likely to be characterized by a degree of formality and conservatism with personal space and independence being valued. In the USA, one of the significant leaders in the external holding environment will be the President; other influences will be much the same as in Britain. Again, in general terms, these are likely to be characterized by informality, directness, competitiveness, and an achievement orientation. In Asia the external holding environments will also include significant leaders and their policies. And, in general terms, these are likely to be characterized somewhat differently by formality, courtesy, modesty, humility, and collective approaches.

These particular and significant people will become internalized mental objects that may be perceived as good or bad largely depending on the particular identity taken by the perceiver. This may also be true of the various formal roles, tasks, policies, and strategies that will also become part of our internal pool of knowledge and feelings. For the most part society may not consist of one homogeneous group but is more likely to consist of several interrelating groups. However, at times of natural crises or at times of threat or extreme joy they may all come together as one group.

Societal internal holding environment

The internal or psychological holding environment that, you will recall, is mainly unconscious, consists of internal objects that are regarded as part of the self and compose the basic social character of the individual. These are derived from life experience, objects that have been previously introjected and will include those currently experienced in our society. These will have commenced with the mental images that we created of our parents or parental figures; a sense of ideals, values, and positive morality that represent a pattern of what to do; and those that represent a sense of guilt and negative morality – of what not to do. These mental images will be added to throughout life, and whether positive or negative may include a significant person such as a political leader, a quality of another person, or a concept. Clearly, these will differ from society to society. However, by a process of self-reflection it may be possible to develop an awareness of your own specific holding environment.

From the perceived view of the societal holding environment, members of society develop a construct of the 'society in the mind'. As in organizations so also as members of society we test reality by comparing our own perceptions and evaluations with those of other persons who experience the same or similar events. The 'truth' of reality concepts is not tested in the isolation of lonely contemplation but in the bubbling cauldron of consensus. I would suggest that the most influential of these groups are likely to be the family and work; or, to put it another way, the family and work (or business) holding environments. This is where we spend the vast majority of our daily lives and this is where we most frequently test reality with others.

We experience the societal holding environment through our perceptive processes and filter them down and match them against the pool of internalized information consisting of our past experience. The various identities that we take will affect our perceptive filters, as will the holding environments that we are a part of. So that, based on current and past experience, conscious and unconscious processes, the internalized multiple experiences result in a construct that we may refer to as 'the society in the mind'. It is this construct of a society in the mind that members of society interrelate with and this leads to the way that societal culture develops. Having developed this construct of the 'society in the mind', the members of that society or part of society then adopt forms of behaviour that they feel are appropriate to them under the circumstances that they perceive are imposed upon them by their societal holding environment. The resultant behaviour is the societal culture.

At the societal level we are still part of a group and still experience society-as-a-whole as if it were the maternal holding environment. And various individuals, but mainly groups, are motivated to act on behalf of society. Thus, we may see Trade Union leaders mobilized to lead the fight against perceived social injustice at work. Or a group of entertainers may be mobilized to lead the fight against perceived injustice and starvation in a foreign country. And a group of antiwar protesters may be mobilized to fight against the perceived wrongness of war and aggression. It will be appreciated that the way that groups become mobilized may not necessarily represent the depth of feeling and injustice that is occurring in that particular group or location, but because they are representing a societal perception it comes with the collective

181

feelings of society. In a previous context the perceived wrong and its associated feelings is displaced on to a particular group.

Organizational culture and change

It is a well accepted notion that organizational and institutional culture is exceedingly difficult to change and frequently has a negative effect on bringing about any change in organizations. But this should not deter anyone, because organizational culture, like personality, is a dynamic process that is constantly changing and is therefore open to change. If we want to change culture we need to understand what component or components of the external holding environment are influencing and bringing about the attitudes and ways of thinking in the internal holding environment. To change the culture we need to change the way the members of the organization view the organization holding environment. I would suggest that one of the main reasons that many so-called culture changes fail is because senior managers fail to reflect and accept that they are the component that most influences negative feelings and the development of a culture that is unhelpful. Too often culture is regarded as a 'thing' and the beneath-the-surface processes are ignored.

In most groups, organizations and institutions the holding environment will be experienced as 'good enough' and the members of the organization will feel as if they are both being held but also being let go, and there will be the sort of basic trust that is necessary for a culture to develop that will positively encourage task performance. However, we will all be aware that cultures have developed in organizations and institutions that have led to their failure. A culture has developed that is negative and does not encourage task performance but may even be antitask. Many of these situations will arise because the members of the organization have experienced the organizational holding environment as evoking strong feelings of abandonment, frustration, or aggressive hostility and hatred. In these circumstances the members of the organization adopt defensive behaviour that they feel is appropriate under the circumstances imposed on them by the organizational holding environment. Put another way, they may unconsciously develop social systems as a defence against the anxiety, as will be described in the following subsection.

3. Social systems as a defence against anxiety

Because the group is perceived at a deeply unconscious level as a maternal entity, we might not think it unusual if the conflicted nature of organizations led to anxiety and that this evokes in the individual primordial struggles similar to those experienced as a child. These may include wishes for fusion and merger as against separateness and loneliness; powerful experiences of satisfaction, nurturing, and frustration: acute ambivalence – emotional (love hate) and defensive (splitting and projective identification); and tensions between engulfment and estrangement. One of the ways that members of groups, organizations, and institutions deal with their anxiety is to develop social systems as a defence against that anxiety. These will then appear as elements in the organization's structure, culture, and mode of functioning.

The natural psychological habitat of man is the group, but man's adaptation to that habitat is imperfect, a state of affairs that is reflected in his or her chronic ambivalence towards groups. Group membership is psychologically essential and yet it is also a source of increasing discomfort. The group-as-a-whole is likely to be viewed by the individual member as an instrument for conscious need satisfaction. This will include a broad range of needs that includes those of an educational or ideological nature. Group associations are also sought to gratify less articulated needs, such as those for belonging, for emotional support, for protection, and for self-help. At the deeper regressive level, the group holding environment can be perceived by the individual as the symbolic representation of a nurturing mother.

Influence of early infancy

The group situation creates such ambivalence and anxiety that it unconsciously returns the group members to earlier relationships with mother and evokes all of the psychosocial mechanisms involved. The elements of this discomfort may be traced back to earliest infancy, where the infant experiences two opposing sets of feelings and impulses, libidinal and aggressive. These stem from instinctual sources and are described by the constructs of the life instinct and the death instinct. The infant feels omnipotent and attributes dynamic reality to these feelings and impulses. He or she believes that the libidinal impulses are literally life-giving and the aggressive impulses death-dealing. At this early stage of life the infant is still part of a dyad and has not yet developed the concept of individuation. The infant attributes similar feelings, impulses, and powers to other people and to important parts of people. The objects and the instruments of the libidinal and aggressive impulses are felt to be the infant's own and other people's bodies and bodily products. Physical and psychic experiences are very intimately interwoven at this time. The infant's psychic experience of objective reality is greatly influenced by his own feelings and phantasies, moods, and wishes.

Through this psychic experience the infant builds up an inner world peopled by himself and the objects of his feelings and impulses. In this inner world they exist in a form and condition largely determined by his phantasies. Because of the operation of aggressive forces, the inner world contains many damaged, injured, or dead objects. The atmosphere is charged with death and destruction, which gives rise to great anxiety. The infant, when faced with such circumstances, uses the mother to reinforce individual mechanisms of defence against anxiety, and in particular against recurrence of the early paranoid and depressive anxieties. This may seem unconnected to group and organizational processes but, as has already been discussed, the group holding environment is experienced at a deep unconscious level as a maternal entity, which means we can anticipate that members of groups will experience the same sort of primordial struggles as those experienced by the infant.

The mother–infant social relationship serves a number of purposes, including the important expression and gratification of libidinal impulses in constructive social activities, as well as social co-operation in organizations and institutions, providing creative, sublimatory opportunities. Many of these beneath-the-surface processes will tend to encourage a positive task supporting culture. However, here in this subsection we are primarily concerned with the effects of a defensive function. When the members of an organization experience the holding environment as being charged with death and destruction and they suffer anxiety, they use the group in the mind to reinforce their mechanisms of defence.

One of the primary cohesive elements binding individuals into institutionalized human association is that of defence against psychotic anxiety. In this sense, individuals may be thought of as externalizing those impulses and internal objects that would otherwise give rise to psychotic anxiety, and pooling them in the life of the social institutions in which they associate. This does not mean that the institutions become 'psychotic'. But it does imply that we would expect to find in group relationships manifestations of unreality, splitting, hostility, suspicion, and other forms of maladaptive behaviour. These would be the social counterpart of – although not identical with – what would appear as psychotic symptoms in individuals who have not developed the ability to use the mechanism of association in social groups to avoid psychotic anxiety.

I have little doubt that most readers are able to recall situations in groups where one or more of those maladapted behaviours have been adopted by individuals or sub-groups. Relatedness between individuals or groups may be strongly influenced by splitting and suspicion. Both emotions and phantasies may affect the way we relate to other individuals or groups. Where, for example, an individual or a group is experiencing negative feelings about another person or another group, such as feeling angry with them or not trusting them, this will affect the way they relate to them. For example, suspicion may lead to the development of a phantasy that one party 'does not care about others' or that one party 'is angry with them because they disagreed with them in the last meeting'. The reality may be somewhat different, but in such cases, it will affect the way they relate to that other person or group. In this instance a likely outcome is that the respective individuals will not have any desire to communicate with the other person concerned for fear of the results.

Collusive interaction leading to external reality

In so far as feelings cannot be worked with personally or institutionally, they are likely to be dealt with by the development of defences against them, and if they are institutional they will come to be built into the structure, culture, and mode of functioning of the institution and thereby impair performance. The danger is that since the anxieties defended against are primitive and violent, defences may also be primitive. A social defence system develops over time as the result of collusive interaction and agreement, often unconscious, between members of the organization as to what form it shall take. The socially structured defence mechanisms then tend to become an aspect of external reality with which old and new members of the institution must come to terms.

An example concerned a health service organization in which the members of the organization, particularly those at admission and ward levels, were experiencing considerable stress and anxiety as a result of an attempt to treat an infinite number of patients with finite resources. The members of the organization who were employed at the interface of the organization and the environment had to cope with what was sometimes an impossible task and experienced feelings of estrangement and abandonment

187

that led to anger and hatred. Over a period of time these feelings were split off and projected into the Director of Administration, who then became an unloved, angry, and hated figure who was the repository of all badness in the organization. As such he was denigrated by the members of the organization and experienced as a really nasty character who could be blamed for all painful experiences.

At the same time, the Chief Executive became the subject of all positive projections and was idealized by the members of the organization. In this way, by locating all painful experiences in the Director of Administration, members of the organization found a vehicle for their own unacceptable feelings. By idealizing the Chief Executive they created a phantasy that this wonderful person would ensure that they were safe and that no matter what happened everything would be fine. This, of course, required the unconscious collusion of all members of the organization, including the Director of Administration and the Chief Executive. The development of the social system, which was used as a defence against the anxiety of trying to perform an impossible task, served to remove from awareness the unbearable thoughts and feelings evoked. However, what it did not do was to deal with the reality of the impossible task. A result was that patients were left waiting on trolleys and a further result was that extreme stress and regular sickness was experienced by staff involved at the interface.

As various group members, sub-groups, or organizational sectors come to symbolize or represent some unwanted aspect, they can serve as repositories for certain projected out elements and are then induced to enact these feelings or phantasies. The often observed patterns of role differentiation, in which groups pressure a member into a needed role, and scapegoating, are comprehensible in terms of projective identification and we can use this framework to understand how people in group and organizational settings use projective identification to cope with complex feelings that arise in the course of ordinary social relations.

A further health service example provides us with a serious warning of the potentially grave consequences of this sort of behaviour; and the need to go beyond a face value view of perceived problems. At a group level, nurses on a ward may find the work so difficult and anxiety-provoking that they suffer from low self-esteem and experience thoughts of extreme incompetence and failure. For a group that needs to remain confident in the face of extreme pain and anxiety, these are unbearable thoughts and feelings. The danger is that they may split these feelings off and locate them in another individual or group. In many wards a convenient location for these split off feelings is the cleaning staff, who may be regarded as different because they are contracted in and are not part of the clinical staff. Should the nurses project into the cleaners these feelings of incompetence they will be left feeling competent again. However, if the cleaners take in the projections and act upon them they will be left feeling incompetent. A serious result may be that they perform as if they were incompetent with a resulting poor standard of cleaning and a huge risk of infection by the 'super bug', formally known as MRSA.

The characteristic feature of the social defence system is its orientation to helping the individual avoid the experience of anxiety, guilt, doubt, and uncertainty. Defences can only be operated by individuals but these are part of group dynamics arising from the notion of the group-as-a-whole. As was described in the above example, a social defence system develops over time as the result of collusive interaction and agreement, often unconscious, between members of the organization as to what form it shall take. An important aspect of such socially structured defence mechanisms is that they are an attempt by individuals to externalize and give substance in objective reality to their characteristic psychic defence mechanisms. In the above example this was achieved by splitting and projective identification. The socially structured defence mechanisms then tend to become an aspect of external reality.

In the previous example the social system as unconsciously developed was given objective existence in the social structure and culture of the organization. As such, it was perpetuated and treated as an aspect of reality, as if the Director of Administration really was bad and the Chief Executive really was good. At one level we might say that the effect of the defence system is to enable the members of the organization in the continuance of the organizational tasks. However, at another level it will be appreciated that it achieves nothing in regard to the original problem that was the source of the anxiety. Thus, while the social system is regarded as real and is an enduring feature of the social structure, it should not be forgotten that it is only in existence as a means of institutionalizing primitive psychic defence mechanisms as an avoidance of anxiety.

Antitask social defences

Unfortunately for task performance, members of organizations and institutions are likely to seek satisfaction of personal needs that are antitask. Such social defences are likely to be antitask as they relate in an unrealistic way. Very often they need to mitigate the stresses and strains of the task itself and of confrontation with the human material on which the task is focused. In other words, members try to establish a social system that also acts as a defence against anxiety, both personal anxiety and that evoked by institutional membership. An example might concern a social service function, such as an old people's home. Doubtless the care of the aged and infirm is a difficult task, especially as many patients will suffer from a decreasing mental capacity and, in the worst cases, senile dementia. Faced with feelings of frustration and helplessness arising from the situation, members of the organization will in most cases deal with this in an understanding manner, treating it as a reality situation and finding ways of owning their feelings. However, there have been occasions when members of such organizations have developed an unconscious phantasy that patients are what might be described as non-humans, and have been denied the usual feelings associated with human beings. In this way the members of the organization blot out any feelings they may have had regarding their patients. A result is that they are no longer working to achieve the organizational task but are working towards a non-caring task that is in fact an antitask.

This sort of antitask social system will appear in all aspects of the institution, both formal and informal, in attitudes and interpersonal relations, in customs and conventions, and also, very importantly, in the actual formal social structure of the organization and its management system. It is also important to appreciate that this is not individual behaviour, rather it is a collusive activity – a total group activity – whereby the individual, group, or sub-group is mobilized by the group-as-a-whole to do something on behalf of the group: they are representing the group. In effect, this becomes the way things are done around here. Or in other words, it becomes part of the organizational culture.

Projection and projective identification

I now want to show how the mechanisms of projective and introjective identification operate in linking individual and social behaviour. Projective identification is an important process that enables us to understand a wide range of group and organizational phenomena. The health service example above provided a description of how this defence mechanism can influence group and organizational behaviour. Projective identification is a frequent occurrence that, we may recall, develops between two or more persons or groups whereby one person projects certain unwanted mental contents on to and into another person or group, with a resulting alteration in the behaviour of the targeted person. It is not just a mechanism of projection, since it also affects another person.

The unconscious transfer of information that occurs via projective identification is primarily a two-phase process. It begins with the denial and ejection of (unwanted) feelings that are inherent in a person's unconscious image (fantasy) of a situation. Let's assume that one group, the senior management group, are concerned about racism in their organization and realize that they may be as culpable, if not more culpable, than others. They deal with their unbearable thoughts and feelings by splitting them off and locating them in the lower levels of the organization. The senior management team, therefore, alter their uncomfortable experience by imagining that part of it is an attribute of something or someone else, rather than of themselves. In the second phase of projective identification, the recipient of the attribution or projection is essentially inducted into the originator's scheme of things. Thus, those at the lower levels of the organization are subtly pressured into thinking, feeling, and behaving in a manner congruent with the feelings or thoughts evacuated by the others.

Here we can see that, while projective identification is a defensive process in the sense of unconsciously serving to insulate the projector from an aspect of his or her experience, it is a mode of communication in the sense that the feelings that are congruent with one's own inner image are induced in another, creating a sense of 'being understood by or at one with the other'. As various group members, sub-groups, or organizational sectors come to symbolize or represent some unwanted aspect, they can serve as repositories for certain projected out elements and are then induced to enact these feelings or phantasies. The often observed patterns of role differentiation in which groups pressure a member into a needed role, and scapegoating, are comprehensible in terms of projective identification.

A work group may divide internally in response to difficult or risky conditions. This division then becomes a social defence: a system of relationships that help people control and contain feelings of anxiety when facing their difficult work. For example, a sales department in an organization may constantly be faced with rejections from customers, this being in the nature of the role. The resulting feelings of incompetence are unbearable and too painful to live with. Consequently, the sales team unconsciously seek out an individual or group that they can split off and project these feelings into. Frequently, this is an administrative or finance team, who are then regarded as incompetent. The sales team can blame all incompetence on the admin or finance team and view themselves as highly competent and able practitioners. This collusive process, which arises out of the extreme anxiety experienced by the sales force, enables the organization to compete by allowing the sales people to conduct their task without fear of failure.

An example of a group scapegoating a sub-group may be the sort of situation where a senior management team cannot deal with the painful thoughts and feelings associated with a failure to achieve the financial goals of the organization. Faced with the possibility of having to make extremely unpopular decisions, such as lay-offs or even closure, they deal with this by splitting off the feelings of failure and locating them in a sub-group such as the sales force, whom they blame for all failings. This group, being one that is constantly living with fears of and actual experiences of failure, are ready vehicles for these projections. This, then, becomes a feature of the organization whereby the sales force are treated in reality as having been the cause of the organization's problems.

Projective identification refers to efforts by persons to rid themselves of certain mental contents by depositing unwanted feelings into another's feeling system. The first person wishing to get rid of an unwanted feeling treats the other as if they had or embodied the feeling state. The way in which the recipient of this process responds has an important impact on the experience of the sender. If the recipient simply enacts the role he or she is assigned, then a tacit, collusive agreement is established in which the original meaning of the unwanted feelings or fantasies is reinforced and the defence against thinking about them confirmed. It will be recalled that if we want to feel good about ourselves then 'not me' has to be bad. We need the other to confirm we are not like that. Thus, the scapegoat takes on or accentuates the characteristics attributed to him or her and confirms the repugnance the other feels for that (disowned) aspect. Perhaps a member embodies the role assigned by the group, such as the rebellion leader.

In many organizations the rebellion leader will be regarded as a trouble-maker, the one who always goes to management with complaints and sometimes with threats of action if so and so is not done or perhaps undone. Seen in the context of the group-as-a-whole this is every bit as much a social system as the other situations referred to in previous examples. Whenever the members of the organization are experiencing feelings of estrangement; a sense of not being all right; of not being nurtured; or, put another way, a feeling that the organizational holding environment is not good enough; they may mobilize the rebellion leader, who is induced to act on their behalf.

The rebellion leader is mobilized to carry and make the painful feelings known to management, who are seen as being responsible for this painful situation and have the power to act to put it right. By mobilizing the individual to act on their behalf, the other members of the group or organization can remain safe from the prospect of driving away their managers, who they need for their psychological and social safety and nurture as if they were mother. I should add that in most organizations my experience has been that the rebellion leader is frequently regarded and treated as a rather stupid person who is a nuisance. I take the view that if management wish to be aware of the feelings of the staff they should listen very carefully to what this individual has to say because he or she is likely to be the only one who is truly expressing the feelings of the members of the organization.

As with culture, it is difficult to provide examples of some of the social structures that are developed as defences against anxiety. The classic example of projective identification is that of the First Officer on a ship who, in addition to normal duties, is held responsible for many things that go wrong but for which he was not actually responsible. The process that takes place is that everyone else's bad objects and impulses may unconsciously be put into the First Officer, who is consciously regarded by common consent as the source of the trouble. By this mechanism the members of the crew can unconsciously find relief from their own internal persecutors. And the ship's Captain can thereby be more readily idealized and identified with as a good projective figure.

Other processes will develop out of the unique circumstances imposed on the members of an organization by their particular organizational holding environment. The forms of behaviour that the members of an organization will adopt will be those that they feel are psychologically appropriate in that organizational setting. What we can say is that members of organizations, acting in an unconscious collusive manner, are likely to make use of all the defence mechanisms that were first developed and used by individuals as defences against anxiety. As with the individual, each circumstance and each use of defence mechanisms will be unique.

We are indebted to Isabel Menzies Lyth for her truly original paper, which describes her ground-breaking work in developing the notion of social systems as a defence against anxiety by nurses in a hospital setting. In brief, she states that the nature of the task of nurses is such that it invokes some of the deepest and most primitive feelings that have their origins in earliest infancy. She then describes how nurses use various defence mechanisms such as denial, splitting, and idealization and avoidance of change to develop a social system that is used as a defence against the unbearable anxiety (see Reading List).

From my own experience of working with police officers, I believe that a similar process occurs in this setting, as I will explain. When police officers join and first take up their duties, they have to learn what it is like to arrest people and take away their liberty. This is an essential part of their role, and as probationer officers they have to display an ability to perform this duty. I would posit that the exercise of authority that results in the deprivation of liberty in regard to those arrested evokes deep and primitive feelings. This may be especially so where partners and children of those arrested are present physically or in the mind. At this stage these feelings are exposed in a raw and undefended manner and may be experienced as unbearable thoughts and feelings. But, of course, these unbearable thoughts and feelings have to be endured if the officer is to perform his or her duties. While not consciously stated or recognized, this first arrest is a sort of social ceremony that marks the passage from outside to inside.

From here on the officer gradually becomes acquainted with the organizational culture and introjects the social and psychological beneath-the-surface processes that are part of the culture. This includes processes that are commonly referred to as 'the canteen culture', which is a form of crude and macho behaviour that is totally devoid of all feelings. Within a short while the process of arresting people comes to be a near routine experience that fails to evoke any feelings. From this, we might well hypothesize that, because of the anxiety concerned with the act of depriving citizens of their freedom, a social system is developed as a defence against that anxiety which involves denial of feelings.

Social systems used as a defence against anxiety are group-as-a-whole phenomena that are part of and highly influence the organizational culture. Such is the collusion and all-encompassing nature of these beneath-the-surface processes that they become an aspect of external reality with which the old and new members of the organization or institution must come to terms. As was explained in the examples referred to immediately above, newly joining nurses and police officers have no choice but to take on the social systems that are in place as a defence against the anxieties experienced in their organizations.

Resistance to change

Earlier, I referred to sentient organizations where we saw culture as a dynamic process that was open to change. However, when social systems as a defence against anxiety are involved as part of the culture they are likely to be highly resistant to change. But, of course, development in institutional functioning is essential in a changing society if we are to ensure effective task-performance. By virtue of its nature, change is inevitably to some extent an excursion into the unknown: it implies a commitment to future events that are not entirely predictable and to their consequences. This will almost inevitably provoke doubt and anxiety in those concerned. Any significant change within a social system implies change in existing social relationships and social structure. It follows that any significant social change implies a change in the operation of the social system as a defence system. While this change is proceeding – that is, while an organization is being restructured – anxiety is likely to be more open and intense. Anxiety and resistance can best be seen as people clinging to existing institutions because changes threaten existing social defences against deep and intense anxieties.

To return to the health service example referred to above whereby the Director of Administration and the Chief Executive were used to carry all bad and all good projections on behalf of the members of the organization, this was a long-established and constantly used social system within the organization. Everybody used the Director of Administration as a vehicle into which they unconsciously split off and projected all painful and unpleasant feelings, with a result that they were now able to locate them in that other person and blot them out of their own experience. If nothing else this provided a process that enabled them to not have to deal with such painful feelings. If this social structure were in some way to be challenged, or made conscious, the members of the organization would need to take back their bad objects that they had been splitting off and own them. As can be imagined, we do not lightly inflict painful experiences on ourselves. But the giving up of the social system used as a defence against their anxiety would have had the effect of precisely that.

The same wide range of social systems as defences against anxiety that have been described in the foregoing paragraphs as occurring in organizations also occur at a societal level. There are a number of society based defences. For example, society's proneness to institutionalize problems felt as too difficult to confront. Society thus splits off the problem, locates it in a small, split-off part of itself, and partially disowns it. The unfortunate result of this is that the institutional caretakers are not well supported, and the quality of care tends to be low. Thus, members of society may split off and disown the problem of having to deal with criminals and all of the associated feelings such as guilt, anger, and denial of their own violent and antisocial feelings. They are then able to deny any association to prisoners and their treatment, leaving the prison officers to take all responsibility while they at the same time are aware that members of society don't care.

Potent figures such as political, business, and church leaders are ready vehicles to attract good and bad projections from members of society. The primordial struggles that we experienced as a child, being still present in our unconscious, will arouse primitive ambivalence whereby we at one and the same time seek the comfort of the dependent position but also seek the freedom of being an individual capable of making our own decisions. When society is experienced as a good enough holding environment; that is, when institutions and their leaders are providing a facilitating environment that both holds us and lets us go, we shall possibly feel comfortable and use the leaders as vehicles for the projection of good objects, such as qualities of goodness and virtue. However, when the societal holding environment is not experienced as good enough and is not providing a facilitating environment for us to be held and to feel secure, we shall possibly use the leaders as vehicles for the projection of bad objects, such as qualities of untrustworthiness or of incompetence.

A further unconscious process that members of groups adopt to deal with anxiety is by regression to what is referred to as 'basic assumption behaviour', which is the topic of the next sub-section.

4. Basic assumption behaviour

Basic assumption behaviour is a much more temporary form of behaviour. Unlike social structures as a defence against anxiety this beneath-the-surface process cannot usually be seen as elements in the organization's structure, culture, and mode of functioning. However, this in no way diminishes the importance of this phenomenon to our understanding of group behaviour. Basic assumption behaviour can incapacitate a group and act as an unconscious means of avoidance of the intended purpose or task. Basic assumptions come into play when the members of the group are experiencing excessive anxiety. When the performance of task is seen as too difficult, and the group consensus is threatened by envy, jealousy, competition, and other unbearable feelings and thoughts, there is a need to find an easier way out.

In all groups there is an interaction between two levels of emotional activity. One of these we may call the work group; the other we may call the basic assumption group. The work group requires an aptitude for collaboration with other participants. In general terms we may say that the work group is concerned with achieving the primary task or intended purpose of the organization and, most importantly, has its basis in reality. The basic assumption group, by contrast, is held together by an automatic and involuntary participation of its members. These may be identified as the mental activities that impede, corrupt, or sometimes support the rational group process. They derive from powerful emotional states that push the faculty of judgement into second place. This is a similar process to that referred to earlier as 'a lack of self perception', but is not the same. The emotional state exists first and the basic assumption state follows from this.

Basic assumption states are viewed as defences against, or reactions to, psychotic anxieties and mechanisms of splitting and projective identification springing from an extremely early and primitive primal scene. If the reality of a group involves facing up to jealousy, envy, and the frustration of dyadic dependency, it is not surprising that primitive fantasies and anxieties may be stirred up. As has been described, by their very nature, groups as the symbolic representation of the maternal holding environment unleash primitive fantasies, fragmentation, and disintegration, and persecution of the bad breast – a world without order and security. What is perhaps not so clear is an understanding of what it was like for the infant at the early stages of his or her existence. But it is this level of understanding that will enable us to gain a deeper understanding of what is behind basic assumption behaviour.

If we are talking about group-as-a-whole activity we can be certain that distant memories of early experiences in the maternal holding environment will be evoked. In this instance we need to go back to some of the earliest life experiences. At birth the infant progresses from a situation of unborn dependence to one of born dependence. In the former situation it is most likely that the infant is under the impression that he or she is omnipotent: that he or she has all that they want and that there is nothing else to wish for. This continues after birth, but now it is achieved in a hallucinatory way. The infant feels him or herself to be in possession of a magical capacity that can realize all his or her wishes by simply imagining the satisfaction of them. At this stage the child makes use of crying and gestures with the same result: that is, satisfaction promptly arrives. During this period the thinking is not in accordance with reality but has all the archaic and magical features that have been described.

We will gather from the above description that basic assumption behaviour is a sort of regression into an emotional state. This is very different from social systems used as a defence against anxiety, where a system develops over time as a result of collusive agreement between group members and eventually becomes an aspect of external reality. Basic assumption behaviour is more like a group regression to the sort of emotional state that we all experienced in the maternal holding environment at the earliest stages of our lives. Now in adult life, as members of a group that is faced with unbearable thoughts and feelings, we regress to an emotional state whereby we feel ourselves to be in possession of a magical capacity that can dispense with these unbearable thoughts and feelings by imagining they have been satisfied.

At this stage, comprehension of the world radiates from instinctual demands and fears. The first objects are possible means of gratification or possible threats; stimuli that provoke the same reactions are looked upon as identical; and the first ideas are not sums built up out of distinct elements but wholes comprehended in a still undifferentiated way, united by the emotional responses they have provoked. Basic assumption behaviour has all the hallmarks of a regression to this stage of human development, behaviour that is aimed at providing solutions to the currently experienced discomfort, based purely on emotions, consisting of archaic and magical thinking, and totally devoid of any relevance to reality.

Work groups

Having described something of what basic assumption behaviour is I shall now describe the separate elements concerned with this beneath-the-surface process. I shall start from a work group situation where the group is engaged with achieving the task for which they have met. In many situations the group may find that their task is one that is perfectly within their collaborative capabilities and continue to work in that mode. The work group mobilizes internal resources and relates to external realities for performance of task. The work group is that aspect of group functioning that has to do with the real task of the group. Whatever the formal purpose or task that the group has met to achieve, be that a planning meeting, a review meeting, or a group employed on an assembly line, the work group can define its task and is actively pursuing its achievement.

By way of example we might consider a management team in an organization that meets regularly to review performance. When functioning as a work group, there may be several identifiable processes that characterize such a group. The members of a work group act in a co-operative manner, each member contributing his or her skill and knowledge. Those present are all willing members of the group who are intent on pursuing the purpose for which they have met. They constantly review and test their progress in achieving their purpose. They are willing to learn from the experience and adopt a creative approach in achieving their purpose. In addition, they will be aware of the necessity to observe the constraints of time boundaries.

In reality we seldom participate in such a wonderful experience, but we do often find that those meetings that we leave congratulating ourselves and perhaps the chair or other group leader all share many of the above characteristics. The fact that these are positive experiences should not cause us to forget that the members will still experience the group at a deep unconscious level as a maternal holding environment. In this particular situation the group provides for and encourages deeply primitive feelings associated with loving, satisfaction, and nurturing. It is a truly idealized situation where the group is credited with all the positive feelings that we associated with the good and nurturing mother.

From work groups to basic assumption groups

Groups that act consistently in this manner are most unusual and, in my experience, unlikely to exist. They may from time to time act in this manner either for whole meetings or for parts of meetings, but to maintain this as a constant position seems most unlikely. The work group, although desirable, may not be achievable, particularly where the task is perceived as difficult or nigh-impossible. Here the members of the group may now be experiencing the task as onerous, and they are perhaps being competitive, envious, and angry to the extent that the resulting anxiety may become unbearable. It is in these circumstances that a further aspect of functioning may occur in the group. When faced with anxiety the group may unconsciously regress to become a basic assumption group

205

that will provide an easier way out. A group that will act 'as if' it were a group met to pursue a basic assumption. At this point it is no longer a work group and is no longer pursuing the achievement of task. It is now in an emotional state that has no connection with reality but is influenced by magical thinking as described above. I should add that this change from work group to basic assumption behaviour is both unconscious and seamless.

In effect, members of the group create a 'basic assumption' by contributing selectively unconscious elements. This anonymous collaboration creates a group mentality that expresses the unanimous but unspoken aims and beliefs of the group. But this group mentality destroys the possibility of any individual privacy. An individual seeking to join the emotional life of a group makes efforts as formidable as an infant seeking the mother's breast. If these efforts are frustrated they regress, and such regression is to the state referred to above where the individual is under the impression that he or she is omnipotent and that they are in possession of a magical capacity that can realize all their wishes by simply imagining the satisfaction of them.

At a social level the members of the group continue to act as if they were adults, and the unknowing observer would barely detect any change in their behaviour. But beneath the surface, when they are functioning in a basic assumption mode they are acting at a deeply unconscious level as if they were in the maternal holding environment, when omnipotence and magical thinking brought them all they needed to satisfy their feelings. All basic assumption functioning has this same quality, but there are variations in the functioning of these groups that can be deduced from observation of such a group. The particular behaviour of the group provides us with the clues as to the type of basic assumption that the group is met to pursue. And this will in turn provide the information that it is not operating as a work group. I should stress that this is a totally unconscious and collusive process that is operating at a group-as-a-whole level.

Three specific types of basic assumption were originally identified, and although others have been identified since, these three remain the most significant. Each of these three types of behaviour can be seen to connect to our earliest experiences. These types of functioning can be observed in all sorts of groups and in all manner of circumstances. They can be said to co-exist with the functioning of the work group and the group may move from one to the other form of functioning. The three types of basic assumptions are: basic assumption dependence; basic assumption fight–flight; and basic assumption pairing, and these are explained separately below.

Basic assumption dependency

In the basic assumption dependency, there is a regression into the state of merging of the early mother–child dyad. Where the basic assumption is of dependence, the group seeks the support of a leader from whom it hopes to receive spiritual and material guidance, protection, and nurture. In this state the group believes that all its needs can be satisfied by one person, on whom it develops total dependence. For this type of group, power is something that is magical rather than scientific; the ideal leader is something of a sorcerer. It will be appreciated that this is very much in line with the period of magical thinking described above.

The aim of the basic assumption dependency group is the attainment of security through one person. The members of the group mentally act as if they are totally without constructive thought or ideas and, despite the fact that they are now adults, as if they were inadequate and immature children. The group treats the leader as some sort of godlike individual who is perceived as omnipotent and omniscient: an all-knowing and an all-doing leader who has the capability of achieving anything and everything. The group may persist in this state for some while, often forming the belief that if they only wait long enough the leader will produce the sought for magic cure. Eventually, the leader will be experienced as not meeting the group's expectations of achieving this totally impossible task. When this happens other leaders may be encouraged to take on the role, but if they do they will all suffer the same fate as the original leader.

In a formal group, such as a regular management team meeting, there are always likely to be situations where conflicting ideas and feelings exist, and these are bound to surface in the meeting with every possibility that the members will suffer ensuing pain and anxiety. In these sort of situations it is likely that the group may regress from functioning as a work group to basic assumption functioning. Where the dominant basic assumption is dependency, a leader will be mobilized to take on the role of protector. This may be the formal leader or one of the other members of the group. A feature of this type of behaviour is that the members will unconsciously perceive who is a ready and suitable vehicle to provide this sort of leadership. There is no actual demand for the individual to become leader, but rather there is an involuntary and instantaneous consideration of the leader taking on the role.

Valency

We may refer to this as valency, which, put another way, is a term that is used to refer to the individual's readiness to enter into collaboration with the group in meeting and acting on the basic assumptions. All of us have a valency to act in one particular way more so than another. We all have a tendency to enter into group life, in particular into the irrational and unconscious aspects of group life in a particular way. Some may have a greater valency towards dependency, others towards fight–flight, and others towards pairing, and usually these will predominate. Individual valency will, in all likelihood, depend upon the early individual experiences of the maternal holding environment.

Basic assumption pairing

In the basic assumption pairing the group is concerned with the aim of uniting. In this state, the discussion will typically become monopolized by two people who seem more or less to ignore the presence of other members of the group. The gender of the couple does not matter, but it does seem to be a kind of sexual relationship. While in this state the group adopts a mood of irrational hope that contrasts with the usual feelings of boredom and frustration, and the group develops a belief that a person or idea will save it by making all difficulties disappear. Again, we will note the link to magical thinking. For the feeling of hope to be sustained it is essential that the 'leader' of the group should remain unborn. It is a person or idea that will save the group from feelings of hatred, destructiveness, and despair, of its own or another group. But in order to be able to do this, it is obvious that the Messianic hope must never be fulfilled.

In the pairing state, two members of the group with a valency towards a notion that everything will be all right and that the world is a hopeful place may take up their role in a variety of ways. The group enjoys the optimism presented by the pair and listen to what is being said with great interest. The group is living in hope of something magical occurring; a new leader; a new thought, or something else that will bring about a new life. Something that will solve all the existing problems and lead them all to some sort of Utopia. It is the feelings or imaginings of hope and optimism that are important to the group functioning in the basic assumption pairing. If a person or idea is produced by the group hope will be weakened. It would appear that the sole aim is to be cocooned in a never ending state of hope and optimism, which may be similar to life as experienced in the womb.

Basic assumption fight–flight

In the basic assumption fight–flight group, members unite to fight or escape from a threat. The group can opt for either activity with apparent indifference – hence the name fight–flight. In this state, group members accept a leader whose demands offer them opportunities for fighting or evasion. They will unite around any proposition that expresses violent rejection of all psychological difficulty or offers means of avoiding difficulty by creating an external enemy. Again, we see the domination of the pleasure principle and of magical thinking that the leader can solve their problems by ignoring reality and adopting a process of fight or flight.

In the fight–flight state, a leader of the group with a valency to fight or flight leads the group into a collusive

functioning that seeks to present itself by fighting someone or something or by running away from someone or
something. The fight leader may lead the group in an
attack on senior management, on another part of the
organization, or on a figment of imagination, an enemy
that only exists as a phantasy. The attack will not be based
on reality, rather all activity will be designed to circum-
vent the task. The flight leader will lead the group into a
flight from reality and, frequently in such situations,
issues will be trivialized and humour will replace any
notion of serious discussion. Basic assumption activity is
never orientated towards reality but involves phantasy that
is then impulsively and uncritically acted out.

Returning to work group activity

Groups can and do alternate from one basic assumption
group activity to another basic assumption group activity.
Thus, a group may move from acting as a dependency
group to acting as a fight group and back again. At some
stage, they may move to or regain contact with reality and
start acting as a work group. We might view basic assumption groups as an interference with the work task, just as
naughty primitive impulses may interfere with the sensible work of a mature person. The work group is a bit like
the serious parent who has a responsible attitude to life;
while the basic assumption group is a bit like playful children who want immediate satisfaction of their desires.
Individuals seem to fear being overwhelmed by the basic
assumptions and develop the need to return to the work
group. It is possible that basic assumption groups not only
develop as an escape from anxiety but also provide an
opportunity for individuals to regain their contact with

reality once the anxiety has subsided after being in the basic assumption mode.

Basic assumptions as temporary social phenomena

It has been suggested that there are two particular organizations where there may be exceptions to basic assumptions being a temporary social phenomenon. These are the church, which may be susceptible to interferences from dependent group phenomena; and the army, which is possibly susceptible to those of the fight–flight phenomena. It is, of course, true that the church mobilizes dependency in a sophisticated way and that the army may represent fight as the motive for battle and flight as the motive for planned withdrawal. In the normal way of functioning these are and need to be reality based activities that are not subject to phantasy, impulsiveness, or acting out. If this were to be the case in each organization this would be seen as a disaster. But it does seem likely that those with a valency for dependency or fight–flight will join the church or army, respectively. Clearly, it is not in the interest of either organization for groups to regress to basic assumption behaviour. Consequently, for each institution to maintain their rational functioning they have to prevent their respective basic assumption groups from being too active or exercising too much influence.

The phenomena associated with basic assumptions are analogous to defences against psychotic anxiety. The more powerful the group's basic assumption, the less it makes rational use of verbal communication. When influenced by basic assumptions the group behave as if they are unable to use symbols. Instead of developing language as a method of thought, the group uses an existing language as a mode of action. When we consider that the regression of members of the group is to a stage before the development of symbols, we should, perhaps, not be surprised that communication is not rational. Basic assumption behaviour is a frequent beneath-the-surface activity in groups, and one which is discernible to anyone who is able to avoid being overwhelmed by the emotions and to stay in touch with reality.

Thus far in this Section we have concentrated on what happens in groups, but have not explicitly explored the boundaries or constitution of groups. Yet, we will be aware that even a random collection of individuals may come together to complete a task of some sort. Given the complexity of establishing what is and what is not a group, it may be helpful to view organizations from a systems perspective.

5. Systems

Systems theory provides a means of studying organizations and their management in a way that facilitates analysis and synthesis in a complex and dynamic environment. It considers interrelationships among systems as well as interactions or relatedness between the system and its external environment. By using the concepts of systems theory it allows us to consider individuals, organizations, small groups, and large groups all within the constraints of an external environmental system. Systems of various types are all around us. For example, we have mountain systems, river systems, and the solar system, which are all part of our physical surroundings. The body itself is a complex organism including the skeletal system, the circulatory system, and the nervous system, and, of course, the mental system. We may also come into daily contact with such phenomena as transportation systems, communication systems, and economic systems. It will thus be clear that we can use the notion of system in various ways.

We may define a system as an organized, unitary whole composed of two or more interdependent parts, components, or subsystems, and delineated by identifiable boundaries from its external environment. Breaking this down, we might start with the identification of a coherent whole. Clearly, an organization might be seen as a system, and parts of the organization, such as sales, finance, and marketing might equally be seen as wholes or sub-parts of the whole.

This type of group or social system is one where groupings of people are aware of and acknowledge their membership of the group. They are, perhaps, most distinguished by virtue of the emotional involvement with other members. Frequently, these groupings develop something of the characteristics of the family: tensions develop, alliances form and reform, and emotions colour the activities. Relating back to our exploration of the group-as-a-whole, such a reaction is hardy surprising given the tendency for groups to evoke memories of and behave as if they were part of the maternal environment.

A basic premise is that an organization, as a subsystem of the society, must accomplish its goals within constraints that are an integral part of the external environment. An organization is an open system that exchanges information, energy, and materials with its environment. Taking this view organizations are dependent for their survival on an exchange of goods and services with their environment

214

and environmental forces have a direct impact on the way the organization structures its activities. The organization performs a function for society; if it is to be successful in receiving inputs, it must conform to social constraints and requirements. Conversely, the organization influences its external environment.

This may helpfully lead us to a systems view that sees organizations as social and psychological sub-systems. The social part of an organization is concerned with the ways in which the tasks of the organization are divided (differentiation) and with the co-ordination of these activities (integration). In a formal sense, structure can be set forth by organization charts, job descriptions, and rules and procedures. It is concerned with patterns of authority, communication, and work flow. This is a relatively simple sub-system that can also be further divided into reasonably clearly demarcated elements such as structure, senior management, strategy, and technology.

When we move to the psychological sub-system we will be aware that every organization is composed of individuals and groups in interaction, and that each will be influenced by psychological factors. These may consist of individual behaviour and motivation, status and role relationships, group dynamics, and other influence systems. They may also be affected by sentiments, beliefs, and values; attitudes, hopes, expectations, and aspirations; the anxieties and defence mechanisms; the ideas and ways of thinking of these same people that both determine how they perceive the external realities and shape their actions towards them. These are phenomena of subjective experience located within the minds of people. Each of these elements may be considered and analysed as a separate element of the sub-system. In addition, we shall need to consider the dynamics arising from the level of the group-as-a-whole.

This is a much more difficult sub-system to define and it is even more difficult to divide it up into its respective elements. Here we are referring to dynamic processes that are unique for each individual or group and for each unique activity. However, what it does do is to call our attention to the fact that in all individual and group interactions the psychological sub-section will have a huge influence on the social sub-system. These two sub-systems – the external and internal worlds of people – are in continual interaction: what goes on in the minds of people is partly reactive to what happens around them, but is also very much proactive. People's ideas and ways of thinking influence the way they act upon their surroundings to bring about change in them.

Systems and psychological boundaries

This also leads us to consider that other wholes may not be as clearly defined. If we take the group of personnel managers referred to earlier in this Section, they may be perceived as a coherent whole by those concerned but this may not be at all obvious to others outside the system. Most importantly, taking a systems perspective provides us with an opportunity to identify and make sense of some of the informal social systems that are present in our organizations. In many instances, nothing on the organizational structure charts will give an indication of this sort of system and those outside the system may not be aware of their existence. By taking a systems approach we may be able to develop the concept of a social system that may lead to a deeper understanding of the dynamics of the organization. When we take a group-as-a-whole perspective it is important that we are able to identify these informal social systems to enable us to discover what they are representing for the organization.

As we have seen, a group can divide in any number of ways and sub-groups may form for any manner of reasons. For example, a group may divide on any or more of the following lines: racial, gender, new members and old members, and old and young, or whatever. In each instance we may view these sub-groups as being mobilized to represent something or to do something on behalf of the whole group. These are all groups that are unconsciously mobilized for psychological purposes. They may be of a temporary nature or more enduring, and each individual may belong to more than one of these sub-groups. Viewing groups from a systems perspective and identifying those sub-groups may be a very rewarding activity.

Boundaries are relatively easily defined in biological and physical systems – they are visible. For example, we can define the physical boundaries of the human body very precisely. But how can we define the sociological and psychological boundaries of human behaviour? To do so we must begin to define this boundary in terms of activities or processes rather than physical structures. Social systems such as organizations do not have any precise physical boundaries although, generally speaking, those activities necessary for the organization's transformation process define its boundary.

Some of the most important boundaries are the psychological boundaries, which define who belongs to the group and who does not. We distinguish external boundaries separating members from non-members, and internal boundaries, in the context of the influence of the group on the individual. That is, we distinguish external boundaries between the 'me' and the 'not me', and we distinguish internal boundaries between the 'in-group' and the others; or between the group and an individual or sub-group who are perhaps scapegoated or in some other way psychologically excluded.

By adopting a systems approach we can expose the fact that what we are dealing with in social system transitions is fundamental change at two distinct levels at the same time, the social and the psychological. It also exposes the fact that the principles by which change takes place at each of these levels are quite different. At the same time, the environmental contexts in which organizations exist are themselves changing at an increasing rate, and towards increasing complexity. This will increase the anxiety on those responsible for the management of organizations as they seek to develop innovative responses. In these circumstances, taking a systems approach may become even more valuable as a means of making sense of that complexity.

This is not least important because this process will expose the beneath-the-surface dynamics that they also need to consider as part of that innovative process. To simply take the view that the formal structure is a rational and sensible process is to deny the fact that the organizational structure is intermeshed with the elements of the psychological sub-system. Simply formulating a structure with strategy and technology in mind and ignoring the psychological needs of individuals may result in anxiety and the development of social systems as a defence against that anxiety which are anti-task.

External influences can bring great pressure on management, who sometimes need to devise responses merely to survive. For example, during recent years many organizations have been forced by fierce global competition to seek to remain competitive by cutting costs. There has followed a huge restructuring of organizations that has frequently resulted in mass redundancies, which in turn affects the job security of those who remain. It has also taken out many management grades by way of introduction of flatter structures, thus removing opportunities for promotion. At a social sub-system level this doubtless seemed a rational response to the perceived problems. However, at a psychological sub-system level this response has been viewed as unfavourable, as the original structure and reward system was perceived by employees as the minimum obligations that they were owed by the organization for their loyalty, conformity, and effort.

The consequences are predictable: employees are angry at the unilateral breaking of the psychological contract, and at the same time insecure, having lost trust in the organization. And their feelings of inequity are increased by the disproportionate benefits enjoyed by top managers, who are perceived as 'fat cats'. Moreover, many feel helpless in the absence of unions or other labour market power to help them to have an effect on the situation. Overall, they have lost their previous feelings of commitment. But such issues of motivation and morale are vital, since lean organizations need effort and commitment to get work done and a willingness to take risks in pursuit of innovation. Here, again, we have a seemingly rational approach to problem-solving that has not taken into consideration the beneath-the-surface dynamics. Given the circumstances, it would not be surprising if an antitask approach was taken by the members of the organization.

To conclude, by using a systems approach we may reconsider the way that members of organizations and institutions set up psychological boundaries to contain anxiety. When members of groups, organizations, or institutions face uncertainty and feel at risk, they set up psychological boundaries that violate pragmatic boundaries based on tasks with the sole aim of reducing anxiety. The boundary separates their psychological region of certainty from a broader region of uncertainty. Or, put another way, they develop forms of behaviour that they feel are psychologically appropriate to them under the circumstances imposed on them by their environment.

Concluding remarks

Taking things at face value, simply reorganizing, changing the structure, or whatever, is one way of dealing with the problems presented. However, when it comes to avoiding and perhaps denying the existence of activity beneath the surface, ignorance is not, of course, bliss. My hope is that I have exposed and explored sufficient of these beneath-the-surface activities to convince the reader of their existence and the important influence they may have on our everyday lives. You may, of course, choose to ignore or deny the existence of these phenomena, but they will still be ever-present and whether you like it or not will be having a constant affect on the dynamics of organizations and other groups of which you are a member. At some stage, if it's not too late, you may need to take heed of what's occurring beneath the surface.

Afterword

In this last part of the book I want to take the opportunity to explore some of the ways that we can develop a capacity to become a more reflective citizen. I feel quite certain that anyone who has read the book thus far will be only too aware that our feelings and emotions have as great an influence on our lives as do our thought processes. In many instances the activity of being a person, that of meaning-making, may evoke deep and unconscious feelings that are primitive and aggressive in nature. If we are to access and gain an understanding of beneath-the-surface activity we need, therefore, to develop a sophisticated level of self-awareness that enables us to control and manage our feelings.

As well as raising awareness, it will also be realized that there are no quick fixes and no short cuts to gaining an understanding of beneath-the-surface processes. You may still be tempted by the latest in a long line of 'how to do it' books and courses, or by the latest fad, but having read and applied this book to your own experience this will now have become part of your own pool of internalized knowledge and feelings, so that when presented with this temptation it may cause you to reject such books as unhelpful. Of course, you may have found this book anxiety-provoking, and have dealt with your feelings of inadequacy by denying that beneath-the-surface processes exist, in which case you may still be tempted. But remaining positive and confident that the book has been a favourable and developmental experience, you may realize that reading books will not provide you with an understanding of experiential learning.

As was stated in the Preface, no matter what our human experiences are they always go beyond our particular methods of understanding at any given moment. There is no methodology that will provide a complete and satisfactory explanation of our behaviour, and the best way that we can gain an understanding of our identity as a self is to look into our experience. By self-reflection it is possible to access much of that which is in our internal private world. And what is more, as human beings we can reflect on an aspect of our past experience and can picture ourselves as doing something; we can recall the sounds; we can smell the smells; recall the touch; and, most importantly, we can then also experience the feelings that we had when we were actually doing whatever it was. Self-reflection, then, is such a highly valuable and helpful tool that we need to hone and develop it.

By reflecting on previous experience we gain a greater depth of self-awareness. Above all, we can understand the emotions attached to our behaviour. The greater the awareness, the greater control we have over our behaviour. The following is a procedure that we can use to enable us to gain a deeper understanding of some of the problems associated with our relationships and relatedness to other people and of those occurring within groups:

- self reflection; leading to
- self-awareness; leading to

- management and control of emotions; leading to
- awareness of others.

It is through self-awareness, leading to self-control, that we can achieve the ability to be aware of and understand others. It should then be possible to have a real and meaningful relationship.

This is not to deny that others may still behave in a manner that causes us concern. It is, of course, true that this may be so, but unless we can gain some degree of understanding as to why they are behaving in this way, little if anything will change, and we shall experience the interface as abrasive. To begin to understand the other person or group requires that we use all of our skills and senses to enable us to gain a fuller and deeper understanding of others. To do so, we need to communicate at three levels as below:

- what we hear (what the other party says);
- what we see (the non-verbal cues that the other party give us); and
- what we feel (the expressed feelings of the other party).

If, as is frequently the case, we rely solely on communication at the level of what people say, we shall miss a vast amount of what is being communicated. Sadly, as non-reflective citizens, this is more likely than not to be the normal situation. But unless we have sufficient self-awareness, as has been shown throughout the book, on many occasions we may not even have control of our own communication, let alone that of others. If we are to truly develop relationships we need to empathize with others and to communicate understanding and acceptance of the other parties at the emotional level, feeling with them.

Taking things at face value, we may be aware of verbal communication in a relationship or between members of a group: what we hear (what other people say). If we are slightly more perceptive we may even be aware of non-verbal communication: what we see (the non-verbal cues that other people give us). However, what we shall not be as aware of (if at all) is an understanding and acceptance of the other party to a relationship or other group members at the emotional level: what we feel (the expressed feelings of others). A reliance on what people say means that we shall miss a vast amount of what is being communicated, with the false belief that we can control our life sufficiently to make its attainment possible.

At a conscious level we can be aware of the emotion being communicated to us through intonations and content of speech. We can also be aware of the level of anxiety by observing the respiration rates and rhythms of the other group members, by studying their facial colouring, their posture, and their gestures. However, it is by using ourselves as a sort of sounding board that we can begin to decipher the responses – that is, the way that we are used and experienced and the feelings evoked in us – that makes it possible to develop hypotheses about the unconscious processes of other people. We can then work with our feelings to identify what is happening in the relationship or in a group, to provide information about differences or commonality, and about what is not being said by the other party to the relationship or members of a group.

A raised level of self-awareness expands the control we have over our lives and with that expanded power there comes the capacity to let ourselves go. The more self-awareness we have, the more spontaneous and creative we can be at the same time. In discovering our feelings it is important that we gain an understanding of the experience that it is us who are doing the feeling; that it is us who are the active ones who own the feelings that we are experiencing. This carries with it a directness and immediacy of feeling, and we can therefore experience the feelings on all levels of ourselves. The more self-awareness we have the more alive we are. Self-awareness brings with it the experience that it is 'me', the acting one, who is the subject of what is occurring and that we feel with a heightened aliveness.

Having an awareness of our own feelings as they occur is the considerable difference between being murderously enraged at someone and having the self-reflective thought 'I am feeling angry' – even as you are enraged. This awareness of emotions is the fundamental emotional competence on which other competencies, such as emotional self-control, build. Without self-awareness we may simply act out our feelings by lashing out at one or more of the others. What we might refer to as blaming, not owning. My experience of working with a variety of people in a variety of settings is that while it is not easy for someone to develop their self-awareness, it is certainly possible. What may make it more difficult in some situations is that others who are aware of their past behaviour may try to mobilize that past behaviour to satisfy their own needs. For example, they might continue to use that person as a receptacle for their projections of, say, anger, whereby the target may find that it is extremely difficult to prevent him or herself from being an angry individual. But this is a necessary starting point, because self-awareness will enable the individual to reject the projections and put them back to the projector.

For all of us, emotional life is in a constant state of flux; we are constantly bombarded by internal and external stimuli that produce continually changing moods and feeling states. These anxieties arise from within and may be may be sparked off by physical stress, painful events, and upsetting experiences. Our ability to cope with these occurrences depends on inner resources and their availability at that particular moment. On some occasions, we may actually rise to a crisis by greater effort and discover unexpected strengths. Alternatively, we may already be strained to the utmost and any additional burden becomes too much. It is likely that there is a potential breaking point for even the most stable of us.

How we cope with anxiety is very connected to having an understanding of these constantly changing states of emotion, which highlights the need for, and the benefit that can be derived from, a trusting relationship between the parties to a relationship or members of a group. Frequently, a party to a relationship or member of a group that is suffering extreme doubts and anxieties will be looking for someone to help them with their pain. By making ourselves available we can provide an outlet and act as a receiver for the excessive anxiety that the other cannot cope with at that time. In doing so, it will give the other the opportunity for the more mature part of them to come to the fore and recover whatever ability they have to understand, work over, and eventually handle the painful situation instead of acting and thinking defensively.

There is much evidence that people who are emotionally adept – who know and manage their own feelings well, and who read and deal effectively with other people's feelings – are at an advantage in any domain of life, such as understanding the processes occurring beneath the surface. Conversely, members of organizations who act on their feelings, for example, by being angry and lashing out when they experience feelings of anger, are likely to be seen in a bad light by others. These people may also have little regard for their own self-worth, whereas people with well-developed emotional skills are more likely to be content and effective in their lives when they understand that it is they who are the active ones and it is they who are doing the feeling. These people master abilities such as:

- being able to persist in the face of frustrations;
- being able to control impulse and delay gratification;
- being able to regulate their moods and to keep distress from swamping their ability to think;
- being able to empathize and to hope.

Conversely, those people who are unable to control and manage their feelings, those people who cannot marshal some control over their emotional life, are frequently engaged in fighting internal battles that sabotage their ability for focused work and clear thought.

Overall, our goal should not be emotional suppression, but balance. Every feeling has its value and significance. A life without passion would be a dull wasteland of neutrality, cut off and isolated from the richness of life itself. What is required is appropriate emotion – feeling proportionate to circumstance. When emotions are too muted they create dullness and distance. Individuals who are experienced by others as 'cold fish' do not inspire; rather, they appear uncaring and uninterested. It is equally true that when individuals are experienced by others as 'raving lunatics' they may, in these circumstances, be regarded as unapproachable. It is only when feelings are owned and

227

expressed in an appropriate and proportionate way by individuals that they will be regarded as inspiring. The first step is self-awareness, catching the worrisome episodes as near their beginning as possible – ideally, as soon as, or just after, the fleeting image triggers our anxiety. To be effective, we need constantly to monitor the cues we receive for anxiety.

Emotional development is needed if the feelings of others are to be recognized and respected. Most stereotypes are based on ignorance or the wish to scapegoat others who are different in some way. Familiarity with those different from ourselves is necessary if these labels are to be overcome, with opportunity to explore mutual feelings in some depth. Before we can relate at an emotional level with others, understand what they are feeling and identify with those feelings (that is, empathize), we have to be self-aware, in touch with and understanding our own feelings. We also need to be sensitive to the non-verbal cues that indicate how others are feeling. This includes tone and volume of voice, eye contact, facial expression, posture, and gestures. It is recognized that it is not what is said but how it is said that really matters. If a large percentage of an emotional message is communicated non-verbally, then skill in interpreting these signals is essential if misunderstandings are to be avoided.

It will be appreciated that we cannot make other parties to a relationship or members of groups change. They, like us, have an internalized pool of knowledge and feelings based on their lifelong experiences. But by gaining a deeper understanding of our own processes we shall gain an awareness of what may be happening to other people beneath the surface. In addition, we can provide the conditions that will increase the chances that other people will choose to change. This requires us to consider both psychological and social aspects of our relationships and relatedness. If we make a serious effort at understanding ourselves in the context of a given situation, trying to see how we have contributed to it – willingly or unwillingly, consciously or unconsciously – then our view of the matter is nearly always altered, as is our manner of handling it. In other words, if we are able to adopt a reflective approach, using the procedure detailed above, we may have a deeper understanding of the situation.

What we are concerned with is the environmental provision that is well adapted to the needs of the individual at any one particular moment. In other words, this is the same subject as that of maternal care, which changes according to the age of the infant, and which meets the early development of the infant and also the infant's reaching out towards independence. This way of looking at life may be particularly suited to the study of healthy development. The psychology with which we are concerned here takes maturity to be synonymous with health. This way of reasoning uses the concept of maturity equated with psychiatric health. It could be said that the mature adult is able to identify themselves with environmental groups or institutions, and to do so without loss of a sense of personal going-on-being, and without too great a sacrifice of spontaneous impulse. Put another way, we can experience this situation as both being held and able to let go. This is the role previously referred to, where the mother needs to hold the infant both physically and emotionally. This holding 'facilitates' the child's mental development because it allows a time span in which to learn to cope with his or her anxieties.

For the infant, and, it is postulated, for all of us in partnerships or groups, the quality of the holding environment is vital. There is a need to develop a sense of security where we will carry around an expectation that we will not be 'let down'. In the organizational or societal holding environment the quality of conditions needs to be the same as in the maternal holding environment if it is to be regarded as a 'facilitating environment'; that is, one that is healthy in the sense of there being maturity; one in which there will be progression. If members of an organization or society are to express themselves in a creative, spontaneous way; if they are not to be overwhelmed by anxiety; if they are to have the confidence to overcome setbacks and still pursue their desires; there is a need for a facilitating environment.

Trust in interpersonal relationships is essential if full and open communication is to occur in a relationship or group. Open non-manipulative sharing of information is required for the effective solving of work or societal problems. This all sounds simple but, as is the position in the maternal holding environment, trust does not exist automatically; it has to be developed from experience. In the work or societal situation, much will depend on the sort of facilitating environment that is experienced. Work orientations that are based on the manipulation of staff generate widespread distrust at all levels. Such distrust of the leader or manager by others is one of the initial problems encountered in any group. Trust is exceedingly difficult to come by and very easy to lose.

An important element in developing trust is listening, which promotes a feeling on the part of others that their problem is being shared, that someone who is genuinely interested in their welfare is helping to work to a satisfactory solution of it. This feeling is symbolized by our frequent use of the term 'we' in discussing the situation with them. The feeling of sharing itself mitigates the burden and eases the tasks that must be undertaken in working towards a solution. This feeling of sharing serves to reinforce the self-esteem of those concerned and with this support they are better able to bear frustration for the sake of future benefit – they develop hope.

In conclusion, I would simply say that when we carefully reflect on our lives, we have a greater appreciation of the less obvious sort of learning that also starts from our earliest days: that which we may refer to as 'learning from experience'. The beneath-the-surface behaviour described and labelled throughout the book, and the many descriptive examples, will have provided the basis for an understanding of the processes and phenomena that make such a huge impact on our everyday lives. But that's as far as this book can take you. As stated in the Preface, when we speak of experiential learning we are referring to our experience, to our learning, which means that we are talking about changes within. For the individual reader to gain the desired deeper level of understanding, it requires that each needs to become a reflective citizen. This may, at times, prove difficult, but I can offer some hope because experiential learning is continuous and constantly changing. In the light of new experience our pool of internalized knowledge and feelings is added to, and in some situations previous categories or classifications of sense data are changed, which demonstrates that these are dynamic processes and shows that change is possible. We can influence our attitudes, values, and belief system positively if by self-reflection we can achieve sufficient self-awareness and understanding.

RECOMMENDED READING

General

Gould, Larry, Stapley, Lionel, & Stein, Mark (2001). *Systems Psycho-dynamics of Organisations: Integrating Group Relations, Psychoanalytic and Open Systems Theory*. New York: Other Press.

Gould, Larry, Stapley, Lionel, & Stein, Mark (2004). *Applied Experiential Learning: The Group Relations Training Approach*. London: Karnac.

Hirschhorn, Larry (1992). *The Workplace Within*. The MIT Press: Cambridge, Massachusetts.

Obholzer, Anton, & Roberts, Vega (1994). *The Unconscious at Work*. Routledge: London.

Section 1

Boundaries

Lawrence, W. Gordon (1979). *Exploring Individual and Organisational Boundaries*. London: Karnac.

Emotions in organizations

Stapley, Lionel (2002). *It's an Emotional Game: Learning About Leadership from the Experience of Football*. London: Karnac.

Defence mechanisms

Freud, A. (1966). *The Ego and the Mechanisms of Defence*. London: Hogarth Press.

Section 2

Relatedness

Miller, Eric J. (1985). The politics of involvement. In: Arthur D. Colman & Marvin H. Geller (Eds.), *Group Relations Reader 2*. Washington, DC: A. K. Rice Institute.

Trust

Stapley, Lionel (2003). Developing trust: obstacles and understanding. In: J. B. Kidd (Ed.), *Trust and Anti-trust in Asian Business Alliances*. London: Palgrave.

Authority

Obholzer, A. (1994). Authority, power and leadership. In: A. Obholzer & V. Roberts (Eds.), *The Unconscious at Work*. London: Routledge.

Hirschhorn, L. (1997). *Reworking Authority: Leading and Following in the Post-Modern Organisation*. Cambridge, MA: Organisation Studies.

Authority, punishment and discipline

Stapley, Lionel (2002). *It's an Emotional Game: Learning About Leadership from the Experience of Football*. London: Karnac.

Values

Kernberg, Otto (1998). *Ideology, Conflict, and Leadership in Groups and Organizations*. New Haven, CT: Yale University Press.

Section 3

Groups

Armstrong, David (2005). *Organisation in the Mind*. London: Karnac.

Ashback, Charles, & Schermer, Victor (1987). *Object Relations, the Self, and the Group; A Conceptual Paradigm*. London: Routledge & Kegan Paul.

Organizational culture

Stapley, Lionel (1996). *The Personality of the Organisation: A Psycho-dynamic Explanation of Culture and Change*. London: Free Association Books.

Social systems as a defence against anxiety

Menzies Lyth, Isabel (1988). *Containing Anxiety in Institutions*. London: Free Association Books.

Basic assumptions

Bion, Wilfred R. (1961). *Experiences in Groups and Other Papers*. London: Tavistock.

Bion, Wilfred R. (1962). *Learning from Experience*. London: Heinemann.

Bleandonu, G. (1994). *Wilfred Bion: His Life and Works 1897–1979*. London: Free Association Books.

Colman, Arthur D., and Bexton, W. Harold (1975). *Group Relations Reader 1*. Washington, DC: A. K. Rice Institute.

Colman, Arthur D., & Geller, Marvin H. (1985). *Group Relations Reader 2*. Washington, DC: A. K. Rice Institute.

Journal

Organisational & Social Dynamics. An International Journal for the Integration of Psychoanalytic, Systemic and Group Relations Perspectives. Sponsored by OPUS.

This bi-annual Journal contains a broad range of related papers on many of the topics covered by this book.

Organizations that provide Group Relations learning (alphabetical by country)

Australia

Australian Centre for Socio-Analysis: www.acsa.net.au

COSG Group RMIT: www.st.rmit.edu.au/cos

Group Relations Australia:
www.grouprelationsaustralia.org.au

Chile

Departamento de Administración, Facultad de Ciencias Económicas y Administrativas, Universidad de Chile: www.facea.uchile.cl

Denmark

PROCES ApS: www.proces-aps.dk

OPU (Education in Organisation psychology): www.iga-kbh.dk/opu

MPO (Masterprogram in Organisation psychology, University of Roskilde): www.ruc.dk

Finland

The Finnish Society for Organisational Dynamics, FINOD: www.organisaatiodynamiikka.fi

The Metanoia Institute, Finland: www.metanoia.fi

France

International Forum for Social Innovation:
www.continents.com/FIIS.htm

Centre International pour la Recherche, la Formation et l'Intervention Psychosociologiques (CIRFIP):
www.cirfip.org

CEFFRAP: http://ceffrap.free.fr

Intistut Français d'Analyse de Groupe et de Psychodrame (IFAGP):
ifagp@club-internet.fr

Groupe d'Analyse en Institution et de Recherche en Psychologie Sociale (GAIRPS):
georges.roquefort@wanadoo.fr

Cercle d'Etudes Françaises pour la Formation et le Recherche: Approche Psychanalytique du groupe, du psychodrame, de l'institution (CEFFRAP):
ceffrap@libertysurf.fr

TRANSITION Analyse de Groupe et d'Institution, Association européene: transition2@wanadoo.fr

Germany

oezpa International, Institute for Strategic Organization-, Personnel-Development and Leadership (Germany):
www.oezpa.de

Holland

Group Relations Nederland: www.grouprelations.nl

Ireland

The Irish Group Relations Organisation:
www.irishgrouprelations.org

Israel

OFEK – The Israel Association for the Study of Group and Organizational Processes: http://atar.mscc.huji.ac.il/~ofek

The Program in Organizational Consultation and Development: A Psychoanalytic–Systemic Approach: e-mail: msfreud@mscc.huji.ac.il

I.C.S – Inovation and Change in society, Israel: e-mail: verred@netvision.net.il

Italy

CESMA – Centre for Experiences and Studies in Management – Milan: e-mail info@cesma.org

Il NODO Group – Training, Consultancy and Research – Turin: e-mail: info@ilnodogroup.it

Spain

Leister Consultores: www.leisterconsultores.com

Sweden

AGSLO: www.agslo.se

South Africa

University of South Africa: www. unisa.ac.za

Turkey

oezpa International, Institute for Strategic Organization-, Personnel-Development and Leadership, Istanbul (Turkey): www.oezpa.com

United Kingdom

The Bayswater Institute, London: www.bayswaterinst.org

The Bridge Foundation, Bristol:
www.bridgefoundation.org.uk

The Grubb Institute, London: www.grubb.org.uk

OPUS, London: www.opus.org.uk

The Scottish Institute of Human Relations, Glasgow:
www.sihr.org.uk

The Tavistock Clinic, London: www.tavi-port.org

The Tavistock Institute of Human Relations, London:
www.tavinstitute.org

University of West of England, Bristol, Centre for Psycho-Social Studies: www.uwe.ac.uk/research/centres/pss/

USA

The A. K. Rice Institute for the Study of Social Systems:
www.akriceinstitute.org

About OPUS

OPUS—an Organisation for Promoting Understanding of Society—was founded in 1975 and is a registered educational charity and company limited by guarantee. Its name reflects its aim, which is to encourage the study of conscious and unconscious processes in society and institutions within it. OPUS undertakes research, organizes conferences, promotes study groups called "listening posts", and publishes bulletins and papers.

OPUS has over 200 Associates, a growing number of whom are from outside the UK. OPUS Associates are mainly professionals from a range of disciplines. OPUS also sponsors the international journal *Organisational & Social Dynamics*, which has a subscription base of nearly 500 throughout the world. In addition, OPUS organizes the Annual International Conference, 'Organisational & Social Dynamics', which is a well supported and valued event.

Through the consulting wing, OPUS Consultancy Services provides consultancy and research regarding individual, organizational, and societal dynamics. The work of OPUS primarily uses an experiential approach to learning, drawing on an extensive history of action research and group relations learning. The resource that OPUS makes available to its client organizations and individuals is guided by two particular principles: all interventions are tailor-made for the needs of each client; and all OPUS consultants are committed to helping clients become more effective in diagnosing their own problems and finding solutions through the transfer of skills and insights.

Further information about OPUS, can be obtained from:

By post: The Director, OPUS, 26 Fernhurst Road, London SW6 7JW

By phone or fax: +44 (0)20 7736 3844

By e-mail: director@opus.org.uk

Or visit the OPUS website at www.opus.org.uk

For information about becoming an OPUS Associate contact Membership Secretary at: membership@OPUS.org.uk.

For information about the OPUS International Journal *Organisational and Social Dynamics*: contact Director as above.

For submission of papers to the OPUS Journal: contact the Editorial Assistant, Organisational & Social Dynamics: e-mail: atbr20906_2@blueyonder.co.uk

For enquiries regarding Opus Consultancy Services and research:

Contact Director (as above).

About ISPSO

The International Society for the Psychoanalytic Study of Organizations (ISPSO) provides a forum for academics, clinicians, consultants and others interested in working in and with organizations utilizing psychoanalytic concepts and insights.

Founded in 1985 by some of the most distinguished contributors to the field, the organization presently has an international membership of over 200.

The society's international three-day annual symposium has been a major forum for thinking about and discussing the application of psychoanalytic theory to organizations. The Symposium has been held in Melbourne, Philadelphia, New York, Paris, Chicago, Jerusalem, Toronto, and twice in London during the past seven years. Many of the papers presented at these Symposia are located in the ISPSO archive on the web site as follows: www.ispso.org

INDEX